To

My "Good
friend" Harry Pawley ;
after 23 years. I will
admit I hate the agony
process but it sure is good
to renew our friendship —

Best Wishes —
Bill Fatz
8-2-73

THE UNITED STATES

vs

WILLIAM LAITE

THE UNITED STATES vs WILLIAM LAITE

W. E. LAITE, JR.

PUBLISHED BY
ACROPOLIS BOOKS LTD. / WASHINGTON, D. C. 20009

ACROPOLIS BOOKS LTD.
*Colortone Building, 2400 17th St., N.W.
Washington, D. C. 20009*

Printed in the United States of America by
COLORTONE PRESS, Creative Graphics Inc.
Washington, D. C. 20009

*Type set in English
by Colortone Typographic Division, Inc.
Design by Design and Art Studio 2400, Inc.*

Library of Congress Catalogue Number 75-184718

Standard Book No. 0-87491-324-1

To little Bill and Kathy,
both of whom were spared the knowledge
that their daddy was a convict.

If
You Wish to
Astonish the World
Tell the
Simple Truth

—RAHEL

1

THE DOOR CLANGED SHUT BEHIND ME. Still dazed by all that had happened in the past few hours, I had difficulty absorbing the scene in the metal-and-concrete room.

Two naked men were seated, facing each other, on the cool, hard floor. They were playing dominoes. Tattoos covered almost the length of their bodies.

Three others were seated on benches, two on one side and one on the other side of a steel table against the far wall, playing cards. One was naked. The other two wore coveralls; they were bare from the waist up, the upper part of the coveralls knotted by sleeves around their midsections.

The remaining man, at the far end of the windowless but brightly-lit room, was black. He was seated on the toilet, and at first I thought he was using it, but then I saw that the lid was down. He was staring at the floor.

None of them paid any attention to me.

Instinctively I pushed back against the door. I realized I had been leaning against it, my hands against the steel bars. I could feel perspiration easing down between my shoulder blades.

One of the men playing dominoes cursed loudly and half rose to his feet. My body stiffened, but then I saw that he had directed the oath at the man in front of him. They glared at each other for a taut moment, then went back to the game.

Remembering warnings I had been given about prison—about how violence and perverted sex games made the days pass faster—my thoughts ricocheted.

I didn't know what to do. My politician's instincts told me to introduce myself, but I couldn't force the words to come. I knew I should sit down, try to appear calm, but I was having a hard time leaving the door.

Finally I moved a few feet down the wall and sat against it.

"That's my place."

The domino player nearest me had tossed the words over his shoulder without looking up from his game. He was huge; his hairy, powerful arms socketed into thick, meaty shoulders. A beer gut bulged out in front of him. His black, coarse hair curled low on his neck and mingled in front with bushy eyebrows. He had not been out of the sun long.

Still without a word, I moved away from the wall and sat down in the middle of the room, about halfway between the white men and the black.

I thought about what my lawyer had told me hardly more than an hour ago, in a court house that now seemed like part of another world: "Whatever you do, Bill, keep out of trouble. Mind your own business, avoid confrontations, and you should be back home in a matter of months."

I thought, for the first time: *My God, is this for real?*

This was what I had dreaded for so long. I had to accept the fact that I was locked up—for how long I could not know—in a maximum security cell in Fort Worth, Texas, thrown in with "common criminals."

And what was I?

I was—or had been—a respected citizen. The closest I'd ever been to a jail cell was as an official visitor. I was a young—thirty-five—and prominent citizen, a former member of the Georgia Legislature.

What was I doing in here with what I considered to be foul-mouthed, sadistic riff-raff? I had an unreasoning impulse to get up, very calmly, walk to the door, and leave. I had to make myself think, believe, *know* that I couldn't. I had to face it—I was trapped like an animal in a cage.

I realized suddenly that something had changed in the room. While I had been trying to organize my thinking, the positions of the other men had shifted. It was a subtle change, and though watching them intently, I had not comprehended what was happening.

They had circled me. The two domino players still had the slates between them, but they were farther apart and closer to me, to my left. The cards were lying unused on the steel table. One man leaned against the bars behind me. Another sat cross-legged in front of me. To my right, the fifth man, no more than a kid but with muscles bulging underneath his tattoos, stood glaring at me, his face set and unreadable.

"Well, well, well . . ."

This was the dark, hairy one. He was holding a single domino with a thumb and forefinger of each hand, gazing at it. "Well, well, now. It looks like we've done got us some fresh meat, don't it now? . . ."

The hard-muscled kid, still staring straight into my eyes drawled, "I wonder where this baby's from."

A voice came from my left: "We'll get this baby tonight. We'll find out just what he's made of."

I felt terror crawling up through my intestines and into my lungs, hampering my breathing.

This was no nightmare. This time I couldn't wake up.

2

MY PASTOR AND I walked the streets of Dallas like two conventioneers waiting for the bars to open. We walked for miles, peering through the brightness of a hot Texas sky at the office buildings, looking in store windows, ducking briefly into museums and libraries.

The Rev. Ted Griner was pastor of the Riverside Methodist Church in Macon, the city where I had three times been elected state representative to the Georgia General Assembly. Macon is also where I owned my own construction company and where I taught Sunday school in that same church.

The next day, I, William E. Laite, Jr.—husband, father, businessman, churchman, Moose, Elk, and yes, even former chairman of the Rosa Taylor Parent-Teacher Association Grounds Committee—would go to prison. No one knew for how long.

Rev. Griner and I had flown out of the Atlanta airport at midnight the night before. He'd paid for his own ticket, and members of the church had paid for mine.

Looking out the window through blurred eyes as the Delta jet taxied down the runway, I saw Marilyn's figure grow smaller and smaller and finally, still waving bravely, disappear. I had no idea when I would see my wife again; or little blond Kelly, now eight; or Jenny, tall, quiet Jenny, twelve going on twenty-one; or our youngest daughter Kathy, living out her childhood in a school for the mentally retarded in Augusta.

We had checked into a motel when we arrived in Dallas, slept briefly, and then hit the streets. About all there was to say to each other had been said on the plane. I was not to appear in court until the following day. So we walked. Rev. Griner bought a book on handwriting analysis, and as we strolled along he was glancing at it intermittently, filling me in on its secrets. He promised to study a sample of my handwriting when we got back to the motel.

"What we ought to do," Rev. Griner suggested, "is find the best restaurant in all of Dallas, and get you the biggest steak from the tenderest steer in Texas."

He didn't say it, but I knew what he was thinking: "It might be quite a while, my friend, before you have a chance to bite into another steak."

Neither of us was familiar with Dallas, so I asked a policeman to recommend a good nearby restaurant. He pointed us toward an establishment which I understood him to call the "Steak and L." We were exhausted, so we flagged a taxi to spare ourselves the three-block walk.

When we got out, I saw that I'd misunderstood the

policeman's Texas drawl. We were at the "Steak and Ale."

Rather sheepishly I asked the reverend if he'd prefer to look for a cheaper place to eat.

"Never mind," he said, "we're both tired. And besides, this is your night, Bill. Let's go on in."

At our table, I glanced around and saw that several others were drinking. Then I thought of long weeks, months, and probably years stretching ahead of me. And I decided to press my luck.

"You know, preacher, if there's anything I like when I'm hot and tired, it's a nice cold beer. You don't suppose they'll have any in jail, do you?"

He took the hint. "Go ahead," he grinned. "I'll look the other way."

My pastor knows all about compassion—that beer was the best I ever had.

The next morning we were up early. I'd slept fitfully, although I'd been dead tired from all the walking we'd done. We had a large breakfast—sausage, four pancakes, orange juice, and coffee—then returned briefly to my room. We knelt for a few moments by the bed for a long prayer, both of us rising wet-eyed.

My attorney was William Fonville. We picked him up at his Dallas office and with him at the wheel of his car we quickly made the thirty-minute drive over the Texas flatlands to Fort Worth.

On the way I asked Fonville question after question: How lenient did he think the judge might be? Would I serve my sentence in Texas? How true were the stories I'd heard about prison life?

For the most part he evaded direct answers. But he did give some hard advice to how to handle myself while in prison.

"There's one primary rule you ought to always keep in mind," he said. "Mind your own business. You'll get into less trouble that way, and you'll get out faster. I've talked to a lot of ex-cons, and they all say the same thing: keep to yourself, keep your nose clean, and you'll get along much better."

I'd already made up my mind to do that. I'd talked to a Macon man who had spent three years in the Atlanta Federal Penitentiary. He had been reluctant to bare his soul to me, but the gist of what he'd said was: "It's the easiest thing in the world to get into trouble in prison. Your best chance to stay healthy and keep a clean slate is to be strictly a loner."

What I really wanted Fonville to do was assure me that the judge had mellowed since our last meeting and was waiting with open arms, eager to let bygones be bygones, impatient to turn me loose and forget the whole thing. I wasn't being very realistic.

A crazy thought kept fluttering through my mind. Couldn't I just say, "Judge, I'm really and truly sorry, and I promise I won't ever do it again," and wouldn't he put his arm around me and forgive me the way my Dad used to do when I was a boy?

We left the car in a parking garage across the street

from the federal building in downtown Fort Worth. I was to appear in the U.S. District Court there at 1 p.m. for final disposition of my case. Already in force against me was a year-and-a-day sentence, a sentence that by law could not be shortened by parole. Other counts of the indictment against me were still to be disposed of.

Most of the people in the courthouse were on lunch break as we entered through double doors and walked down the wide hall toward the courtroom. I saw a familiar figure approaching.

Leo Brewster hardly fits the image of a kindly, forgiving father. Neither does he fit the stereotype of the leonine, white-maned judge. That day, dressed in suit and tie during a court recess, he looked more like a construction worker in his Sunday clothes—short, stocky, with square-rimmed glasses, apparently in good physical condition for a man approaching sixty, exuding the same stern demeanor with which he ruled his courtroom.

He was cordial, though, as we met in the hall. He greeted Fonville, then turned to me. "Mr. Laite, how are you?"

I mumbled something in response, remembering how unfeeling the judge had appeared as he almost nonchalantly handed down my year-and-a-day sentence several weeks earlier.

Fonville and I both started to introduce Rev. Griner to the judge. It seemed important that my pastor had seen fit to accompany me all the way to Texas. Judge Brewster only nodded and strode away.

We walked into the carpeted, mahogany-and-marble courtroom and took seats on a bench on one side. The people who ran the court—stenographers, bailiffs, clerks—began to drift back in. I recognized most of them, having seen them often during my trial. Most of them now seemed to be avoiding looking at me. A gnawing apprehension was growing. Something told me I was about to get the shaft thrown into me the way Ahab gave it to the great white whale.

Court reconvened but there was another sentencing to take place ahead of mine. The defendant was brought before the judge in handcuffs. His name was Johnny Ray Smith, and his capture had taken him off the FBI's "Ten Most Wanted" list, a classification he had earned by masterminding a nationwide auto theft ring.

In disposing of the case, Judge Brewster asked Smith if he had anything to say. Smith launched into a loud harangue against the judge, the FBI, and law enforcement in general.

I was not only shocked at his lack of respect for the judge, but fearful of what effect Smith's behavior might have on my own case. I felt like the innocent on-deck hitter who has to get into the batter's box and duck a high, hard one just because the preceding batter hit a grand-slam homer.

Smith eventually got around to a point-by-point evaluation of conditions in the county jail, from which he had just departed. Judge Brewster interrupted him once to advise him to clean up his language, but then allowed him to complete his criticism.

Smith said he had refused to come out of his cell earlier in the day until guards let him shave and shower. He complained of poor food, filth, and harrassment by the guards. He said several of the men in his cell, including one disabled veteran, needed medical attention but couldn't get it.

When he finished, Judge Brewster sentenced him to thirty-five years in prison. But he told Smith he would direct a U.S. marshal to look into the situation at the jail.

What Smith had said about the jail had shaken me.

My case was next. The judge briefly reviewed the facts.

At issue was work that my firm had done under a contract to rehabilitate sixty houses in a Federal Housing Administration project in Big Springs, Texas. Principal charges were that I had failed to pay overtime to some employees, that all terms of the contract had not been fulfilled, and that some government property at the site had been stolen or misused.

A federal jury in July, 1967, had returned two indictments totaling twenty-eight counts, charging me with twenty-three counts of irregularities in connection with the work, and five counts of perjury in connection with statements I had made to a grand jury investigating the case.

I had pleaded innocent. On May 17, 1968, a jury convicted me on two counts of perjury. The jury acquitted me on one count and was deadlocked on another, and still another count was dismissed by Judge Brewster.

The year-and-a-day sentence had been on the perjury conviction. What remained now was a final decision on my sentence by Judge Brewster. The agreement between opposing counsel and my counsel was that I would plead guilty to one of the twenty-three counts in the indictment and the other twenty-two would be dismissed. I entered a guilty plea to a charge of making false statements which, the government alleged, prevented me from having to pay overtime wages on some 1,200 hours of work by my employees in Big Springs.

I pled guilty. I was tired of fighting the charges, and my money was gone. I had decided against further appeal of the case after the Fifth U.S. Circuit Court of Appeals upheld my conviction by a lower court.

My own emotions about what I had done were somewhat mixed. I felt, as my attorneys and I argued in court, that I had not violated the letter of the law regarding overtime work and pay. At the same time, I felt in my heart that I had probably violated the spirit of the law. I had gone beyond the borderline of the law's intent.

Judge Brewster asked me if I had anything to say for myself and I stood, but before I could get anything out my attorney grabbed my arm and pulled me back down. He felt that it would be better for me to keep my mouth shut after the previous defendant's blast.

Judge Brewster gave me a dressing down. He said he expected more out of me—a college graduate, a businessman and respected citizen—than he did out of many who appeared before him. He emphasized the seriousness of perjury.

"Mr. Laite, there was just no sense in your committing perjury," he said.

Then he pronounced sentence. He gave me another year-and-a-day sentence on the charge of making false statements, to be served concurrently with the perjury sentence. But then he gave me a break. In a major modification, he changed the sentence to what he called an "A-2," making me eligible for parole. Otherwise I'd have had no prospect of spending any less than the whole 366 days in prison.

When Fonville had asked whether the government attorneys would accept a motion changing the sentence so that I could be eligible for parole, the government lawyers had objected. But Judge Brewster ruled in my favor.

The judge said something about placing me in the custody of a U.S. marshal and then, with a swish of his robes, left the room.

The marshal, dressed for the role in string tie, cowboy boots, and tight-fitting trousers, took my arm to lead me away. I shook hands with Fonville and Rev. Griner.

The marshal led me silently to a small room in the back part of the building. There was a holdover jail cell there, and Smith was in it. He began yelling for the marshal to bring him something to eat, citing his constitutional rights. While the marshal was handcuffing me, he asked if I wanted something to eat, too, and I asked him to bring me a sandwich.

He left, and a minute later Fonville and Rev. Griner came through the door. I was delighted to see them; I'd thought they had already left.

They asked me how I was doing.

What could I say? "Okay, I guess."

They asked if there was anything they could do for me.

"Bill," Fonville said, "it's painful any way you look at it. But you just keep your chin up, and you're liable to be out in no time at all."

I asked him to call Marilyn for me. "Tell her I'm all right, and not to worry about anything. Tell her I'm pleased that my sentence was modified, and to pray for a parole."

They left me then. I hated to see them go—it would have been easier if they hadn't come back at all. I didn't break down, but I felt awfully full and tight.

Smith had been quiet until they left. He seemed completely relaxed, leaning sideways against the bars of the cell door. "Where you staying tonight, buddy?" he asked me now.

"I don't know," I said.

He chuckled. "I'm staying at the Holiday Inn."

I thought: "You aren't afraid of anything, are you? And, right now, I'm afraid of everything."

The marshal came back in with sandwiches and soft drinks. He let us take our time eating before he finished

22

the job of shackling me. My hands were already cuffed in front. He added light legirons, then wrapped a chain around my waist, threading it through my handcuffs. Smith was already in the same condition. A deputy marshal joined us, and the two of them ushered Smith and me outside to the sidewalk.

I finally mustered enough courage to ask the marshal where we were going.

"The county jail," he said.

That was what I'd been afraid he'd say.

I swallowed the dryness in my throat. "For how long?"

"Oh, a day or two," the marshal said. "We have to wait for word from the Bureau of Prisons on where they want us to send you."

Our little caravan moved slowly along the sidewalk in the midday heat. Smith and I were forced to take short, choppy steps because of the legirons.

I stared past my chained hands at the sidewalk, avoiding the stares of passing pedestrians and motorists. I was beginning to feel the shame of being a convict. I felt like a birddog that slinks along with his tail between his legs after he's been punished.

I felt wronged, mistreated—here I was going into custody several years after the offense had allegedly occurred. The punishment seemed unrealistic and severe. I felt I had been punished enough already—by the publicity and the harrassment, by the financial drubbing that had my family economically drained.

I wondered what would happen at the jail. Surely the guards wouldn't rough me up. Or would they? Surely they wouldn't take advantage of my helplessness. How many other prisoners would be in the cell with me? What would they be like? Would I have anything at all in common with them? What would I do to pass the time?

As our slow journey continued, I thought of what might have happened had I been allowed to turn myself in at Macon. I didn't think the process would have been so humiliating, even though it was my hometown. I remembered that when I was arrested, rather than make the arrest at my home—which would have been the ultimate humiliation—the U.S. Marshal simply called me and told me to come down to his office, at a time that was convenient for both of us. I went through the full arrest procedure—the fingerprinting and all the rest—but it was done more or less in private. In Macon the Bibb County Jail is only a block from the federal courthouse. Here we had gone about five blocks and were still walking. During the long walk I was extremely conscious of the people looking at me, and it appeared to me that almost everybody in town was watching. This many people never seemed to be on the street in Macon.

All kinds of thoughts were skipping through my mind. What were the newscasts saying about me at home? Would I be degraded by the reporters who were probably even then typing their stories? And I wondered how my family was holding up.

However, a persistent thought was overriding all the

others: How could I get out of this situation? What could I or my attorney do to get me out? I was getting desperate. I wanted something to happen fast. As smart as my lawyer was, he must be able to come up with a last-second grandstand play to save me. Up 'til now I'd always been fairly lucky. I wanted to contact Marilyn and tell her to plead with my attorney to do anything in the world he had to in order to free me.

I even envisioned, after the judge changed the sentence to make me eligible for parole, that I would be out for good in a couple weeks. My mind couldn't accept that it wouldn't happen.

"Well, there she is, boys, Your home away from home."

The marshal's words interrupted my reveries. Looming ahead was a tall, modern building with no visible windows.

"That's the Tarrant County Jail," the marshal said.

3

HOW HAD I reached this point in my life?

To begin, I was born in Tampa, Florida, in 1932. During the depression my parents headed north, hunting for anything better, and they made it as far as Valdosta, Georgia.

I grew up in Valdosta—a moderate-sized town in the heart of the tobacco belt in southern Georgia. I never worked in the tobacco fields, but that was one of the few jobs I didn't have.

I was taught to respect and obey my elders, and to work hard. I mowed lawns, packed watermelons, graded tomatoes, milked cows, and planted crops. During World War II I worked my own Victory garden daily.

Later, as a teen-ager, I worked on a number of construction projects, particularly during the summers. This probably had something to do with my decision much later in life to go into the construction business on my own.

On several occasions my mother thought my employers had overpaid me. She would insist that I take the money back. This I would do obediently, red-faced because she seemed to be saying I hadn't earned all the money, and I thought I had.

My parents taught me many of the things I still believe in—say what you believe and believe what you say; tell the truth, even if it hurts; if you're wrong and know you're wrong, admit it and pay the price.

Faced with the choice of going into the Army or working my way through college, I chose the latter. My family had little money, so I earned more than 90 percent of the cost of attending the University of Georgia. I worked in a beer joint and on the college farm while obtaining my B.S. degree in agriculture.

My job on the college farm paid very little, but each morning I would gingerly make my way through the dung droppings in the cattle and hog barns to feed the animals and clean their stalls. To save on laundry bills, I wore a pair of old jeans cut off at the knees each morning. I would then wash the excrement off my bare legs with a hose before changing clothes and going to class. But the scent of my work was not so easily washed off, and it invariably accompanied me to the classroom.

I learned then how victims of discrimination feel. I was an outcast. If I arrived early to class, other students would sit at least four seats away from me in all directions. If I arrived late and sat near any of them, they would twist and squirm the whole period.

Marilyn and I were married while we were at the University of Georgia and my grades improved immediately.

The first job I had after graduation was with Triangle Chemical Company in Macon.

The job meant a great deal of traveling all over the state and the opportunity to meet a good many people in politics. I began to wonder how hard it might be to be elected to the Georgia General Assembly, and what I would be able to accomplish there.

I went into politics for a number of reasons. I'd always enjoyed talking. In college, between the working and the studying, I'd relished a sharp exchange of views on campus government, state and national government, and politics. I usually took the opposite view from whoever started the discussion, especially if he happened to be a prospective lawyer.

On occasion, the words were sharp between a certain pre-law student from Atlanta and myself.

"The fact is," he would say, "laws are what government and politics are all about. And who's the most qualified to make laws and see that they're enforced—a lawyer, whose livelihood depends on knowledge of the law? Or a businessman who sits behind his desk all day—or chases his secretary around it—and never thinks about the law until he gets caught drunk driving home from the Christmas office party?"

And I'd shoot back, "You're wrong—on two counts. Government's not just laws, it's people too. And people are more important than laws. That's why laws sometimes have to be amended, reshaped to fit the needs of the people who elect the lawmakers. Memorizing a lawbook isn't going to help you understand the problems of the farmer, the bricklayer, the small businessman. You've got to understand and empathize with these people to legislate what's in their best interests. A businessman who deals day in and out with people is in a hell of a lot better position to represent them than a slick-dressing lawyer who stops off at the courthouse for a few minutes between the golf course and the country club."

"And another thing—" my voice would be rising by now—"how can you possibly say a businessman doesn't have to know anything about the law? The way things are regulated nowadays, the businessman who doesn't keep right on top of legal precedents is going to wind up in hot water with the Internal Revenue Service or FBI, or one of the other agencies that tell you how to run your shop."

This was a sore point for me, because I'd already looked into the legal requirements for organizing my own business and had been flabbergasted at the amount of red tape involved. I had worked with the FBI during the summer and had run across several cases involving technical violations of the law by apparently conscientious, honest businessmen.

A few years after I went to work there, I began testing the political waters in Bibb County. Some of my business contacts were familiar with the local political parties and voting trends, and they thought the time might be right for a fresh face—especially a non-lawyer. All three of the county's representatives in the House of Representatives were lawyers.

Meanwhile, my son Bill had been born during my last year in college, followed two years later by Jenny. Kathy was next—she suffered brain damage during birth, and the responsibility on my wife was becoming too great. I had to arrange a way to spend more of my time at home. This seemed an opportune time to quit my traveling job and go into business for myself, something I'd already decided to do sooner or later. So I took the state board examination for structural pest control, passed it, and formed Town and Country Pest Control, Inc.

We would not be able to keep Kathy at home much longer. The only public facility for mentally retarded children in Georgia was Gracewood State School and Hospital in Augusta. But there was a long waiting list, and our little girl's name had been on the tail end of it for months.

Something needed to be done to provide additional public facilities for such children, and I vowed to give this top priority if I ever got into the General Assembly.

After weeks of agonizing over the decision, I finally made up my mind. Two days later the *Macon Telegraph* announced that I was tossing my hat in the ring to run for the Assembly, opposing the incumbent, Rep. Phil Taylor, an attorney.

Taylor later decided not to run for re-election, and shortly thereafter I made my first real political enemy. My campaign manager suggested I ask Taylor to publicly support me, so I went to see him.

Taylor countered my request for his support with a question. "First I want to know why you chose me to run against. There were two other posts you could have run for."

"Do you really want to know?" I asked him. "Now, don't ask me a question if you don't want to know the answer."

"I want the answer."

"Well, I qualified against you because in my opinion you were the weakest incumbent."

I didn't get Taylor's support. I suppose I should have given him a more diplomatic answer, but, after all, I was new to the language of politics.

I won the election with 11,936 votes. My closest opponent collected 9,719.

The future was full of promise. Business was good. More jobs were coming in all the time, and the publicity of my campaign was bound to attract more customers. Our family had never been closer; Kathy's illness had drawn us protectively around her.

My political horizons seemed unlimited—already I was raising my sights, considering running for a statewide office once I had proved my worth in the House of Representatives.

The one thing no one ever imagined was that I would wind up in a federal prison.

4

THE TARRANT COUNTY JAIL is a modern-looking mass of steel and concrete towering above a street corner in downtown Fort Worth. There are no telltale bars visible from the outside; a passer-by could easily mistake the structure for an office building.

It is a maximum security facility. Most of the inmates are hardened criminals. Mixed among them, however, are some first-offenders and some repeaters with minimal offenses, being housed there temporarily before movement to a permanent prison.

The jail had about five hundred occupants on that November day in 1969 when Johnny Ray Smith and I, both in shackles, accompanied by two U.S. Marshals, approached it on foot from the U.S. District Court a few blocks away.

We stood across the street, waiting for the light to change. Some of the shock of my sentencing had worn off during the walk, and was gradually being replaced by a mixture of apprehension and despair.

This was the same jail Smith had complained so bitterly about to Judge Brewster.

We crossed the street and encountered elaborate security precautions even before we were allowed to enter the building. We were entering a walkway-driveway at the basement level. A feeling of utter helplessness overcame me as we entered the building. The marshals hovered over us as if we were going to attempt to escape.

We entered the rear of the jail building. There was a telephone hanging on the wall right before the tunnel entrance. The marshal on the right side picked up the telephone and called inside to the security guard, who then instructed the main gate guard to raise the entrance gate which allowed persons on foot or in a vehicle to enter the tunnel security area. After we went through, the door automatically closed.

The closed-in feeling hit me hard, adding to my frustration from being subdued by handcuffs, chains, and leg-irons.

Even in the security area, precautions were strictly carried out against any possible escape attempt. I knew I was not going to try anything and was completely passive. The prisoner next to me, however, was arrogant and loud mouthed. He used every opportunity to insult the marshals and prison officials. His attitude concerned me, because I felt that the first chance they had to subdue him, they might take a crack at me, too, just on general principles.

I could not believe that I had lost my case and been taken into custody, but now in jail I felt that anything could happen. I kept telling myself that when the guards saw me they would recognize me as a good and decent person. It was not long before I realized that the guards couldn't care less what kind of person I was. I soon learned the complete disregard the captors have for the captured—disregard for the prisoners' feelings, well being, or safety.

This impersonal processing reminded me of stockyard sales where farmers brought livestock to be auctioned. The personnel at livestock yards have more concern for the cattle and hogs than the jail and prison personnel have for prisoners.

We came to another door, and one of the marshals gave Johnny Ray Smith a savage shove toward it. The door opened by electronic eye, just before Smith would have slammed into it, and he stumbled to the concrete floor inside. The marshals laughed at this, ignoring his curses as they yanked him up from the floor. I shuffled through the door as fast as I could.

We were separated then, and I was taken to a desk sergeant, who was sitting behind a desk in a steel cage that separated him from the prisoners. Several guards and other personnel were in the large caged-in area, including some clerks and a trusty (an inmate who is "trusted" and has the run of the jail) in a white convict's suit. The desk sergeant was obviously an old hand at processing incoming prisoners, and the tone of his language indicated that he meant to be treated with humble respect.

"We've got two good ones for you," the marshal who was with me said. "Be sure to put this one in a good tank," pointing to me.

I had no idea what a tank was, but what I imagined was far from good.

The desk sergeant asked the marshal if I could be trusted and perhaps be considered for a trusty, and when the marshal answered affirmatively, a little hope was raised in my mind. Again I asked how long I would be there before being transferred to a permanent institution, and again the marshal told me it would be no more than a couple of days.

I was too overwhelmed by what was happening to ask many questions—it had taken a good deal of courage to ask how long I would be in the jail.

A black officer of the jail was instructed to search me, and he took both my hands in an abrupt way and placed them on a wall as high as he could. Then he kicked my ankle indicating for me to move my feet backward, placing me in an unbalanced position which was awkward and uncomfortable. I was so upset that when he hit my ankle it did not seem to hurt, but later I felt it and realized that it was badly bruised. While I was in that stance, he checked my pockets and my body for any concealed weapons or other objects.

The desk sergeant then directed me to take everything out of my pockets and place it on the desk. He told me to remove my wristwatch, college ring, and wedding ring. I realized that my wedding band had never been removed, and I didn't want to remove it then, although I couldn't show my feelings. It didn't make sense for them to take the ring. After it was off I kept looking at the untanned circle on my finger and thinking of Marilyn.

About that time another jail guard ordered me to follow him. I started walking along behind him, but he stopped suddenly and said, "Wait, you haven't been in the holdover yet."

He took off my manacles and marched me a few steps to a holdover cell, a room with solid walls on three sides and bars in front. There must have been about forty prisoners inside, most of them crowded toward the bars. They all began talking and yelling as the guard and I approached. The guard had to beat them back with his billy club in order to pull the door open and shove me inside.

Most of the men seemed to be drunks right off the streets of Fort Worth. They crowded around me, asking for a drink or a cigarette, and I pushed my way through them to the back of the cell. The filth and the stench were overpowering. My shoes slipped on the spit, vomit, urine, and cigarette butts on the floor. I pressed against the back wall with my hands in my pockets. The others in the cell looked miserable, and most of them appeared to be either drunk or on drugs. The cell echoed with their begging and hollering. I could not believe the scene, which was completely foreign to anything I'd ever experienced before.

After what seemed like hours, the guard returned and yelled for me, and I quickly shoved myself through the sweating bodies and pawing hands to the door. My clothes—business suit, white shirt, and tie—were rumpled and damp with perspiration caused by the heat of the bodies in the cell and by my nervousness as well. I stood face to face with the guard at the door, and he asked me, "Have you had enough of that?"

I didn't understand what the guard meant until later when I realized that this was part of the game for the prison personnel. They are prisoners, too—the only difference is that after eight hours they get to leave the prison for awhile. They amuse themselves by placing the inmates in various situations to see how they'll react.

The guard led me into a small room where hundreds of wire baskets were stacked up with piles of gray-black prison coveralls with "TARRANT COUNTY JAIL" stenciled all over them. The guard told me to strip down, throw my clothes in one of the wire baskets, and put on a pair of the coveralls he thrust toward me. They were too big and baggy, and the legs piled up on my shoes. I timorously suggested that I try on another pair, but the guard snapped that he didn't have time "to be coddling law violators."

We went back to the desk sergeant and I was given four one-dollar bills and a dollar's worth of change. The sergeant explained in his gruff way that the commissary sent someone around once a week with candy, cigarettes, and other items.

A different guard took me then, and we went into the prison elevator. It had bars down the center, separating the guard and me. From that moment on, there were always bars between the guards and me.

By this time my spirits were very low, and I was weak from the shock of the experience. Everyone was a stranger to whom I was nothing more than a nuisance, and I began to realize that I was in for a rough time.

The elevator reached the seventh floor, stopped, and the door opened. I entered one side of a caged-in walk area, still separated from the guard. Everything seemed to be operated electronically. I could hear the clanging of distant doors as we got off the elevator and began moving down the divided hallway.

I was placed in another holdover cell, but only two prisoners were in this one, and both were lying on the floor asleep. They were both black and tough looking. I stood near the door, carefully not making any noise, hoping against hope that they would not wake up. I wondered how they could sleep when the noise of the steel doors and other sounds were almost splitting my eardrums. The air was cold, and as I stuffed my hands in my pockets and stood there waiting, the suspense of what was going to happen rubbed my nerve ends together like an electrical short circuit.

Before long the guard reentered the area just outside the holdover cell, with a trusty. The jail door opened, and the trusty entered and threw some things on the floor at my feet. The guard hollered, "Pick it up." I jumped noticeably at his sharp command and then reached down and picked up a plastic cup, a towel, a blanket, and a sheet.

"Okay, let's go," the guard said.

We left the holdover cell and walked down the hall to a thick door resembling the doors that separate water-tight compartments of a submarine, but this door had no wheel to spin to open it.

The door opened, and the guard directed me to step inside. He closed that door, and I was standing alone in a small enclosed area, all steel. The guard watched me through a small, thick glass view-window in the door. He electronically opened the next cell door. "Go on through," he said, now speaking into a microphone at-tached to a sound system that magnified his voice, making it bounce loudly off the metal walls. I stepped through the next door and was in a narrow corridor with a number of cells along the wall to the left. On the right, glancing through bars into a large room, I noticed several prisoners sitting around, some with their clothes partially or com-pletely off. The guard told me to go down to cell number five, which was just ahead.

This cell was very small, with solid steel on three sides and steel bars facing the front. The door slid open.

"Put your stuff on the bunk."

I entered and put my blanket, towel and cup down as directed.

"Now, come back out."

I moved back into the corridor, and the cell door,

mounted on wheels along runners, slammed shut. The corridor was about three feet wide. This time a door on the other side of the corridor slid open. "Go ahead," the guard ordered, and I went through the door just before it slid shut with a bang.

There were six men in the room. At the end of the room where I had entered, five white prisoners were playing cards or dominoes or lying around watching the players. A black man was sitting on the toilet stool on the opposite side of the room near the end to the left.

The six men had been convicted of crimes ranging from robbery, aggravated assault, auto theft, rape, to murder. I was two years older than the oldest man in the room, but from the standpoint of the only kind of experience that counted at the moment, I was a child. All had been behind bars at least twenty months, and one for twelve years—more than a third of my lifetime.

This was the tank's "dayroom."

The concrete floor was painted bright red—*blood red,* I thought in horror. Two steel benches and a table built into the far wall were green; everything else was steel gray. There were no windows. Lights built into the ceiling flooded the long room. Other than the one table and the benches, there was no furniture. Toward the end of the room was the commode on which the black man sat. It was actually a commode-sink unit set against the opposite wall, and next to it was a shower stall. The room was approximately twelve feet wide and thirty-five feet long.

For several long minutes I stood where I was, trying to maintain my composure. The appearance of the men revolted me. Their attitudes baffled me. They had to know I was in the room; the guard's voice had echoed through the whole seventh floor, yet no one even glanced up. Their nakedness and semi-nakedness was something I had not expected, and I found it blatantly, almost savagely, offensive. The tension in the air was almost tangible enough to feel or smell.

I was overwhelmed by my absolute helplessness. I could not leave; I could not run away. I was locked in with these men. I was suddenly afraid with despair I had never before known.

I thought from looking at them that these men were different from me in a very basic and dangerous way. While I had been convicted of a white-collar crime, they had committed crimes of violence. I didn't know how to act. I'd always been able to adapt to any situation, but I'd never faced anything like this. The last thing I wanted them to know was that I wasn't as tough as they were, but I was afraid to act the part.

Their language was filled with obscenities—every other word was foul.

The five men nearest me were young, but looked hard.

My eyes kept going back to their tattoos. One man had "sweet" over one nipple and "sour" over the other. Another had a female's genital parts tattooed around his navel. There were tattoos of naked women, tattoos of men's sexual organs, tattoos of rings and watches, swastikas, and U.S. flags.

Finally, I moved down the wall and sat down on the floor. One of the domino players muttered, "That's my place." So I moved to the center of the room and sat with my arms around my knees. Gradually the five of them gathered around me and began baiting me.

"Where's this dude from?" one asked.

"I wonder if he's got any guts? Well, we'll find out tonight, won't we?"

"Reckon what her name is?"

"She looks ready for about six or eight inches."

"You figure she'll make us fight for it, or is she gonna give it to us nice and sweet, like a good little girl?"

"Naw, prob'ly we'll have to work her over a little first. But, hell, that's half the fun anyway, ain't it?"

I couldn't move. I was terrified. This couldn't be real; it couldn't be happening to me.

Then I heard the electronic doors sliding open. A moment later the door to the dayroom opened, and a young boy stepped inside. He couldn't have been more than eighteen, a slender boy, with longish brown hair and thin-rimmed glasses that gave him the appearance of a college student. His prison coveralls, like mine, were sadly oversized, making him appear all the more forlorn and vulnerable.

The attention of the other prisoners at once turned to the boy. He stood uncertainly as the door rolled shut, nervously looking around the room. Then he went to pieces. His head dropped forward, tears sliding down his soft cheeks from beneath his glasses.

Out of the corner of my eye I saw a movement that didn't make any sense to me. A hairy, dark-skinned convict had pulled off a shoe and sock, and he was stuffing bars of soap into the sock. Suddenly he moved, springing cat-like toward the boy, swinging the sock in a long sidewise arc at the back of the boy's head. The kid crumpled limply to the floor.

They were on him at once like jackals, ripping the coveralls off his limp body. Then, as I watched in frozen fascination and horror, they sexually assaulted him, savagely, brutally, like starving animals after a piece of raw meat.

Then I knew what they meant when they talked about giving me six or eight inches.

How many of the men raped him, I don't know. I witnessed the whole thing, but it was a blurred conglomeration of changing images in my mind—as if I were catching glimpses of an incredibly obscene movie while driving past a drive-in theater in the rain. I know that all of them did not take part in the attack, but neither did any of them try to prevent it.

Neither, of course, did I.

One of them pulled several pencils out of his pocket and passed them around. They set fire to the erasers with matches one of them produced from a pants pocket. Then while one of them mounted the boy, the others jabbed his arms and neck with the smoldering erasers, causing the boy's unconscious body to twitch and jerk. When one of them had trouble entering the boy, he took soap and water and lathered himself, and another stood behind him and shoved.

Finally they finished. The last one to molest the boy shoved his thin body flat against the floor, and in a final sadistic gesture, shoved his fingers deep into the boy's rectum and ripped out a mass of bloody hemorrhoids.

As the nausea hit me, I dashed toward the commode but never made it. Half way there the vomit came spewing out of me, splashing on the red floor. The black man hadn't moved at all; he still sat on the closed toilet, tapping his foot to a silent tune, looking straight ahead, eyes unfocused.

Afterward, as the boy lay there, the odor of the sweat and blood and semen almost made me vomit again.

I hid my face in my hands and prayed for the nightmare to end.

5

FOR SEVERAL MINUTES AFTER THE ASSAULT, the young boy lay unconscious. His attackers had gone back to their dominoes and cards as if nothing had happened. The black man still sat unmoving, seemingly unmoved, on the toilet.

Except for his socks, the boy was naked. His glasses had been shattered when he'd hit the concrete floor face-first, and a broken lens had opened a gash over his left eye. The blood was seeping down his face onto the red-painted floor. I cringed against the back wall, filled with revulsion, but also with pity for the boy. But I also knew a sickening sense of relief that it had happened to him instead of me. His arrival on the scene was all that had saved me. They had raped him rather than me only because he was younger and easier prey.

At the same time, I had to come to grips with my shame and guilt. Why hadn't I tried to help the kid? Why had I sat there, numbed, watching, doing nothing?

I could tell myself that I could no more have prevented what had happened than I could have turned back a herd of raging elephants—and I knew this was true—but it did little to soothe my guilt.

This wasn't the outside; different rules applied here. My lawyer and several others had warned me repeatedly to avoid getting involved. Hadn't they told me that was the best way, the only way, to stay out of trouble, keep a clean record for the parole board?

The boy was beginning to stir. He raised his head, looking dazedly around him. I could see full awareness of what had happened coming into his eyes. He buried his head in his arms, his thin body shaking with sobs.

Then a commotion of some sort outside filled the dayroom. I could hear voices, the rattling of dishes.

"Come and get it, you dogs!"

The voice came through a small opening about knee-high in the wall at the end of the dayroom where I had entered. The inmates began moving in that direction, one or two of them pulling their coveralls back on. One kicked the kid's outfit in his direction. As the black man walked past the boy, he tossed a roll of toilet paper to him. Red-eyed, obviously in great pain, the boy sat up weakly and began gingerly stuffing wadded tissue paper between his bloodied legs.

Mealtime. 4:00 p.m. I had been in jail less than two hours.

The men began lining up as the food was passed in to them through the small opening. The boy lay on his side against the wall, his eyes closed. I went over to him, tapped him on the arm, asked if I could get him some food. He lashed out viciously at my hand. "Don't touch me," he snarled. For all he knew I could have been one of his attackers.

I got the last tray of food. Turnips, starchy lima beans, and stale bread. I knew that if I ate it, I would not keep it down. The others were sticking their cups through the slot, then pulling them back in, filled with coffee. But I had left my cup in my cell.

Sometime later an ear-splitting bell sounded, the dayroom door opened, and men began filing out, moving into their individual cells. Again I tried to help the boy, who was limping toward the door, supporting himself weakly against the wall. He cursed at me, jerking away. So I went out the door and down to my cell.

A minute later, the doors to all the cells slammed shut. We were locked in for the night.

For the first time since entering the dayroom, I felt safe.

I dropped down on the bunk, weak, physically and emotionally drained. Macon, my wife, my two daughters—they seemed an eternity away, and here I was, locked in with vicious criminals. Would I ever again see my home, my family, all the things that were so familiar and had been taken for granted for so long—would I ever see any of them again?

I was on the edge of hysteria, panic; and I knew that to give in to it, to allow myself to break down, was the last thing I could afford. I was certain that if I showed any sign of weakness, the boy's attackers would be on me like dogs. Working on a farm as a boy, over and over again I had seen chickens picking out the weakest member of the brood and then going after him relentlessly—pecking at him, pecking, pecking, until finally, weak and bloody, he died. The same rules apply in jail.

I got down on my knees beside the bunk and prayed, silently, tearfully, finally closing the prayer with a supplication that the Lord's will be done—hoping that His will was for me to get out of this place alive and unmolested.

I stretched out on my back on the bunk, hands behind my head, and clearly sorted out my thoughts for the first time that day. One thing was definite: I had to plan what to do. I couldn't just rely on chance.

The marshal had said I'd only be in jail for a day, two at the most. Perhaps I would get out tomorrow. Surely a permanent prison would have to be better than this—despite what I had heard about the Atlanta penitentiary and some others.

In the meantime, I had to protect myself. The best thing to do was to put up a tough front. Try to psyche-out the other inmates. Make them think I was something I wasn't. After all, they knew nothing about me. For all any of them knew, I might be another Dillinger, or a nightclub bouncer, or an ax murderer.

By the time I finally fell asleep, I had convinced myself that I could make it until the marshal came back for me. The sounds of inmates in other cells drifted into mine—cursing back and forth, banging on the walls and bars, snoring—for what seemed like more than two hours. It must have been well after midnight before I dozed off into a tossing, troubled sleep.

I woke to the sound of a bell, grabbing my ears, trying to shut out the deafening noise. It took me a second or two to remember where I was. Then I saw the steel bars, and glanced down at my jail uniform, and all the fears and doubts came flooding back, filling me.

I hardly had time to rekindle some of the courage I'd fired up the night before when the cell door slid open. I followed the rest of the men back to the dayroom, hating to leave the safety and seclusion of my own cell.

Just as we got inside the dayroom, a guard's voice came over the loudspeaker, jolting me as I heard a name that sounded like mine. "Where's Laite?" He pronounced it "Latey."

"Laite?" I said. "Here. I'm right here." I stepped back out into the hall so I could see the guard peering through the view window.

"Son, you'd better get that mop and broom and clean up this hall, and be damn quick about it! Don't you know it's your day?"

I saw one or two of the other prisoners grinning as I

squirmed and tried to explain that I hadn't known it was my turn, or even that the hall was supposed to be cleaned. Apparently the job alternated among the inmates, but I didn't see how I could have been expected to know this.

"Shut up, Latey!" he snapped. "One more word, and you go into the hole!"

I didn't know why he was so angry, and I didn't know what "the hole" was, but I didn't ask any more questions. I got the mop and broom and went to work.

Later, in the dayroom, there was breakfast—if that name can be applied to a single slice of unevenly toasted bread and a tin cup of stale coffee. Again the boy didn't eat. He lay on his side, moaning, obviously still in agony. He obviously needed medical attention. Why hadn't something been done for him? Certainly the jail officials had some method of surveillance that included the dayrooms. But, if they did, then why hadn't a guard intervened when the boy had been attacked?

I began considering the possibility of getting word out to a guard that the boy needed to see a doctor. I didn't know how to go about it, but there must be a way. Right now, though, I had to worry about my own safety.

I took the four one-dollar bills and the dollar in change from my pocket. Carefully, deliberately, I laid it down beside me on the floor, placing the bills neatly one atop the other, then stacking the coins on the bills. I saw a couple of the other prisoners looking at me with vague curiosity. Three others were napping on the floor. The silent black man was back at his station on the commode.

After a few minutes went by, one of the men got up and casually walked over to me. He stood there for several seconds, looking down at me. I didn't look up.

"What you in for?" he asked finally.

I looked up at him blandly. "Life," I said.

He stood there for a long moment, looking down at me, then glancing over at the money. Then, with even greater nonchalance, he walked away.

It was pure bluff. I hoped they'd get the idea, from my deliberate placement of the "bait" and from my "life sentence," that I knew how to handle myself and was more than willing to prove it to any doubters. I wanted them to think I was daring them to start something.

The money seemed to fascinate them. All throughout that day, they would shuffle past, one by one, staring at the neatly piled bills and change. One cursed the money under his breath as he passed. Another kicked at it, but didn't quite let his foot touch it. None of them, in fact, made contact with the money—not even when I left it lying there while I went to the other end of the room to use the toilet.

But the dark-skinned one, Mike, began shaping up during the day as the one who would have to try me, sooner or later. The others seemed to be afraid of him and did his bidding without question. They brought him drinks of water, gave him cigarettes on demand. One of them obediently combed and braided his long, coal-black hair pig-tail style for him.

After a time, Mike began feeling me out, badgering me from a distance.

"I got a feeling the dude there is gonna cause us some trouble," he'd say. "I reckon we'll just have to straighten him out, won't we now?"

Then later, in a conversational, almost friendly, tone, he'd ask, "Say there, dude, I wonder how a tough guy like you would stand up to my bolo punch, huh? I mean, you got a little padding there around the gut, so, who knows, you maybe could live through it. But suppose I aimed just a little lower, how you reckon you would take that?"

"Why, Mike, you mean old thing, you just might injure the dude permanently," one of his yes-men would snicker, the others grinning, watching intensely.

"That's all right. Hell, he'd still be useful the same way the kid was."

I sat against the wall, staring past him, pretending total indifference to all of them, but I was afraid of what could happen if they ever got up the nerve to call my bluff. Beneath my jail clothes, I was sweating with fear; on the outside, I tried to appear calm and cool.

"Remember the last dude we had in here?" Mike went on. "Now he looked a lot like this dude. Acted a lot like him, too—sort of stuck-up and smart-assed. Remember how we learned him some manners?"

"Naw, Mike, I forget. Remind me," one of them said, as if on cue.

"We softened him up a little bit first," Mike said. He was sitting on the table, completely nude, feeling with his left hand sizable biceps on his right arm. "We belted him around, bounced him off the bars a few times. Then when he couldn't get off the floor, we kicked him around a little—you know, kicking him where it would do the most good."

"Did he learn to be good?" It was the same man asking the question, a short, muscular, pie-faced one.

"Yeah, he did. After he quit crying and bawling, he promised us he'd act a lot better from then on, and sure enough, he did."

He kept up his taunts off and on, the rest of the day.

In a situation like this, the effect of the tension, the constant mental punishment, on the nerves is awful.

In the outside world you can avoid insults, fights, even accidents to some extent, by being careful or by simply walking away. In jail you can't. You can't walk away. You can't get out. And you can't know how you'll react, if you'll be equal to the challenge or not, until you come face to face with it.

Throughout the long day, I kept waiting for a guard to come and tell me a U.S. Marshal was there for me. But the day wore on and on, and when a guard finally came and called my name, the exultation that rushed up through me was wasted. He wasn't there to take me out of the tank.

Instead, he brought me my first communication from the outside world. And it got me into trouble.

It was a telegram from two good friends, Charlie

Norman and J. W. Arnold. Addressed to "HON. WILLIAM E LAITE," it read: "JUST HEARD THE GOOD NEWS LOOKING FOR YOU BACK SOON HAVING A LITTLE KNOCK." It was signed with their initials.

The guard who brought the telegram to me seemed furious about the way it was addressed. "You're not honorable, Laite," he shouted at me. "You're dishonorable. You're a sorry damn convict; you're a good-for-nothing jailbird, and you'll get along a whole lot better if you remember that!"

He demanded an explanation of the message. "It sounds like some kind of code. Are you trying to pull something over on us?"

I explained as best I could that Charlie and J. W. had apparently learned from Marilyn about the change in my sentence that made me eligible for parole. This was the "good news" they were talking about. A "little knock," I told the guard, was our term for having a little drink.

He stalked away. From his attitude, I doubt that he believed a word I told him.

Despite the difficulties, I was glad to get the telegram. It boosted my spirits, at least for a while, to be reminded that people remembered me and thought enough to send a message.

I was still concerned about the boy who had been attacked. His name, I had learned, was Danny. If the marshal did come for me, I was planning, on my way out, to tell the guard or desk sergeant everything that had happened the day before, so that Danny could get medical attention and his attackers could be punished. But no marshal came.

Late that afternoon, however, the chaplain came by. He talked through an intercom at one of the three visitors' windows on the same end of the dayroom where the trusties brought the meals.

The men crowded around, bombarding him with complaints—about the food, the guards, the temperature in the cells, and anything else they could think of, real or imagined. They broke up as the bell rang to send us to our cells for the night.

I lagged behind for a second and whispered to the chaplain that the kid on the floor needed a doctor. Danny was just beginning to agonizingly pull himself to his feet.

I didn't know whether the chaplain heard me, or whether he'd believe me, since he obviously heard so many complaints that were without substance. But he would have to notice the way Danny limped when he left the room.

Apparently he did. Early the next morning two guards came and helped Danny walk out of the dayroom between them, one of them telling him they were taking him to a hospital. One of the inmates called loudly to Danny as he moved slowly down the corridor: "Remember, you'll be coming back!"

I couldn't believe that. I was certain the boy was out of the place for good. I wondered what would happen to the men who had raped him after he told about it—if any telling was necessary in light of his condition.

Meanwhile, Mike resumed his verbal attacks as I took my seat against the wall, carefully arranging the money beside me. I continued to ignore his remarks, as if he were beneath consideration. But on the inside I was trembling.

Mail was delivered every morning. The letters were placed in a slot at the end of the dayroom. I'd noticed the day before that nobody moved to get the mail until Mike gave an order. At that point, whomever he named would bring the mail to him, unopened. Mike would open most of it before passing it on to the owner.

One of the letters he opened this day was addressed to a prisoner named David, who sat, flushed but still, as Mike tore open the envelope, laughing. Mike tossed the envelope to David but retained the letter. "Well, now, I wonder what sweet things Betty Lou is going to say to me today?" Then he read the intimate letter aloud, while David sat in helpless mortification, squirming but saying nothing.

The letter was from David's wife. It told how much she missed him, how she lay awake in bed at night thinking about him, wishing he were there so that she could hold him and feel comforted and secure.

Mike got a big laugh out of that. "Now why would she want a little punk like you in bed with her when she could have a real man like me?" he asked, fondling himself.

Still David said nothing, and Mike tossed the letter to him. David picked it up and stuffed it inside his shirt, biting his lip.

Mike picked up the next letter in the stack. "Well, I'll be damned," he said. "Here's one for the dude."

I jumped to my feet and stood there, tensed, staring at him from several feet away, waiting to see what he would do. I had been hoping for a letter, but fearful of what might happen if I got one.

Mike opened the letter. "It's from someone named Marilyn," he said. "Who's that, dude? Your wife? Or your shackup? Don't be bashful, you can tell us."

The others snickered nervously, watching me. I was trying to restrain myself, to get control of my thoughts. I didn't want to tangle with him—even if the others didn't back him, he looked as if he had been fighting all his life, and he was considerably bigger than I was—but I knew if he started to read Marilyn's letter aloud, I'd have to challenge him.

I stared back at him. He watched my face for a moment. Then he glanced over the letter cursorily, first one side, then the other. Finally he threw it at my feet. The whole room was quiet.

Mike cleared his throat. "It's a lousy letter anyhow," he said. "No sex in it at all."

He was quiet for a while after that. But later in the day he resumed his badgering of me.

I also got my first letter from my mother that day. For some reason, Mike passed it on without opening it or commenting on it.

I read it and Marilyn's letter over and over while the

rest of the men were eating lunch. It was one of the few times during the day when general tranquility reigned in the cellblock.

Both letters dampened my eyes. I hoped the other prisoners, especially Mike, didn't notice.

Marilyn was obviously trying to be cheerful, to pep me up, but it was obviously a strained cheerfulness. She recounted everything she and the girls had done for the past twenty-four hours, filling the pages with chit-chat, stressing that they were fine and would continue to be fine, demanding that I keep my chin up and not worry about them.

"Not that we can keep from worrying about you," she said in closing. "But let us do the worrying, not you. We love you and miss you very much."

Shortly after the noon meal, a guard brought Danny back. I couldn't believe it. Why on earth had they brought the boy back to this same cell? Didn't they know he would be exposed to the danger of another attack by the same men? The whole thing was insane.

Gradually I was beginning to understand that this was the way the place functioned. The people who ran the jail didn't care what happened to the prisoners. All they cared about was avoiding anything that might interrupt the smooth operation of the jail. Assigning Danny to another cell would have been more trouble than putting him back into the same one; it would have meant extra paperwork for someone.

It was obvious, too, that nothing was going to be

done to the boy's attackers. Had he known he would be placed back in the same tank, he probably would have not even told about the attack, being afraid of retribution.

These prisoners had been locked up for breaking the law; but here in jail a serious and brutal crime had been committed and it was going unpunished.

The idea was to isolate the criminals to protect society from them. Never mind protecting them from each other.

That evening after supper, Danny's sister came to see him. They had to talk against a background of obscenities shouted by the other prisoners. In vivid language, they described what they would like to do to the girl. Mike and another prisoner, both fully dressed for a change, exposed themselves to her.

I went back to my cell that night more shaken and depressed than ever. There was no way of knowing how much longer I would be in jail. Three days had passed now. Each day I seemed to be getting closer to a showdown with Mike. I had already swallowed more of my self-esteem than I'd ever have thought possible. I trembled at the thought of what might happen if I did clash with Mike, because I was sure the others would take his side. But I knew that the longer I accepted his insults, the less credence I would have in my role as a hard-nose.

The two letters had come at a time when they were badly needed. They had helped greatly to boost my waning courage.

Alone, finally, in my cell, I read Marilyn's letter again

and again, visualizing just how she must have looked as she sat at the kitchen table, where she wrote all her letters. It had probably been late at night, after Kelly and Jenny were in bed, on the night I'd entered the Tarrant County Jail. Bill Fonville would have called her that afternoon, told her where I'd been temporarily lodged, and given her the good news that I was eligible for parole.

There were splotches on the letter, blurring the ink, which I knew were tear stains.

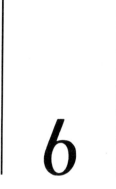

I BOUNCED INTO THE STATE CAPITOL in January of 1963. I was a typical freshman representative—a bit brash at times, but showing the proper deference to the old veterans of the House and Senate; trying to learn all the intricacies of the Legislature as quickly as possible, and trying to get to know personally as many of the representatives and senators as I could.

I would bet, and give odds, that nobody ever loved politics any more than I did. I thrived on it, all of it—the parliamentary maneuvering on the floor of the House, the heat of debate, the give-and-take as sponsors of bills tried to line up enough votes for passage while their opponents bargained hotly for the same votes, the wheeling and dealing that went on when the House was not in session. Much of this took place in the old Henry Grady Hotel, several blocks from the Capitol on downtown Peachtree Street in Atlanta, where many of the lawmakers lived during the forty to forty-five days of annual legislative sessions. Here, late into the night, representatives from Ty Ty, Ludowici, Ball Ground, Macon, and Atlanta would crowd into one of the rooms where the smoke was thick and the liquor flowing, where many important bills were born or buried right there.

On my first Sunday in Atlanta as a legislator, I was drawn into a function that I later learned was held regularly on the fourteenth floor of the Henry Grady. I wandered into one of the larger rooms where twenty-five or thirty lawmakers were gathered, sitting around in chairs, on beds, sprawled on sofas, smoking, drinking, joking back and forth. Over in one corner, in discussion with three of them, was a lone female, a very striking blonde, flashily dressed.

Pretty soon one of the men came around, holding a hat in his hands. "Okay, Laite, let's have your money," he said, as if I knew what he was talking about. I didn't, so I asked.

As he explained it, the program would go something like this: All the male guests would drop money, along with a slip of paper with their name on it, into the hat. Then, informally, the money would be presented to our honored guest, the blonde. Then, aided by one or more of the gentlemen, she would step up onto the desk which had been shoved to the center of the room, and would perform for the edification and aesthetic pleasure of the male audience what is sometimes referred to as an exotic dance.

"But the names in the hat," I asked. "What about them?"

He then explained that at the end of the dance, after grateful acknowledgment of her applause, the young lady would reach into the hat, pull out a slip of paper and read aloud the name.

"What happens then?" I asked.

"What happens then," he whispered into my reddening ear, "is that the dedicated public servant whose lucky name is chosen is offered the honor of what is sometimes referred to as a 'date' with the attractive blonde for the rest of the evening."

On this particular night, though, my friend explained, there was a bit of a snag. He wondered if I could help. I said I would be happy to try.

The young lady, he explained, was holding out for more cash—poor child, she had a sick old mother to support. Would I be so kind as to go out into the halls and recruit some more male guests, making sure each one brought a dollar along?

I said I would.

However, no sooner had I stepped outside the room, than I spotted a newspaper editor, whom I knew casually, coming my way. I ducked back inside. I could visualize the front-page expose—my name in glaring black type. I breathed a silent prayer that the editor hadn't spotted me.

He had. He came into the room. "Hi, there, Bill," he clapped me heartily on the back. "What's going on?"

I made some inane response, feverishly trying to figure how I was going to wriggle out of this one. I hinted that perhaps we might move down to my room and discuss the vicissitudes of the newspaper game. He said he didn't much care to, thanks all the same. "Say, now," he asked, "why do you suppose that young lady is getting up on the desk there, Bill?"

I said that I had no earthly idea.

As his mind became occupied with the flowering festivities, I eased away from him and located the legislator holding the hat. Luckily, he was one of the few men in the Assembly whom I knew rather well. I explained my predicament and suggested that, unless he wanted to share billing with me in tomorrow's headlines, he should lend me the hat for a moment, names and all. He gave in without argument.

I began removing the slips from the hat, trying to make myself inconspicuous in the corner of the room. But I needn't have bothered; no one was paying even the slightest attention to me. The young lady had a way with the audience. I tore off a dozen or more new slips of paper and wrote the editor's name on all of them. The applause and yelling were approaching a crescendo, so I knew I had to hurry. I elbowed my way back up near the desk and returned the hat to its caretaker.

When the moment for the name-drawing arrived, the blonde, to more cheering and applause, bent over cutely and withdrew a slip from the hat. She unfolded it and read out the editor's name, loudly and clearly. Everyone began looking around for him.

The editor was a man who was seldom at a loss for words but this time he was struck dumb. He recovered fast, though, and allowed as how, due to the pressure of an early deadline, and with appropriate apologies to the young lady, he would regretfully have to suggest that another name be drawn.

So the attractive blonde drew another—and another—and then another—and by then the newsman knew he had been had. He took the joke in good spirits, though, and I knew as he left the room, laughing good-naturedly, that there was no longer any danger of an expose.

During my first few days in the House, still puffed by my election victory, I was eager to tangle with the biggest, toughest opponents I could find. Carl Sanders seemed a perfect target. The sauve, handsome young Georgia governor, a stunning victor a year earlier over old-line segregationist Marvin Griffin, had reached the point in most governor's administrations where the state budget catches up with the campaign promises. Sanders had to have more money, and that meant more taxes. He announced his program for a substantial tax increase, promising that most of the revenue would go to improving state schools.

I had campaigned on a platform opposing any tax increase.

I contended that there was some fat in the state budget that needed paring, and that the money already coming into the treasury, coupled with more efficient operation of state government, ought to be sufficient.

"Laite Raps Gov. Sanders' Tax Bills," a *Macon News* headline blared. And a few days later, *"Laite Takes New Slap at Sanders!"*

I had met the governor only briefly, at a reception for new legislators at the governor's mansion. So I was flattered one morning during session when a Sanders' aide tapped me on the shoulder and handed me a note as I sat at my House desk. Written in the governor's own hand, the note read, *"Bill—Please see me in my office immediately. Carl Sanders."*

I showed the note to a veteran representative who sat on my right. "Looks like old Carl's ready to do some horse trading," I grinned. My friend read the note, a slow smile growing on his face. He offered no comment.

Downstairs in the governor's outer office, I was greeted by about a dozen other representatives, most of whom I recognized as being first-year men like myself. One or two of them held pieces of paper that looked much like the kind my note was written on. We sat there, not saying much to each other, as the minutes ticked past. Before long several of us were up on our feet, nervously pacing the small room, trying to work up enough nerve to go into the next room and ask the governor's secretary what the delay was.

I had almost made up my mind, when the secretary strode briskly in. "Gentlemen," his smile was gracious, charming, "I'm afraid I have some bad news for you. Gov.

Sanders has been called out of town unexpectedly. He asked me to convey his regrets to you for this inconvenience, and to tell that he'll talk with each of you later."

I was a little annoyed, but even more, I was disappointed. I'd been looking forward to a face-to-face confrontation with the governor. I'd felt that I might be able to impress him with the logic of my arguments against his tax measure.

Back at my desk, I saw that the old-timer on my right was smiling more broadly now. "Well, did you and old Carl get things all hashed out between you?" he asked innocently.

"No," I said. "Something came up. The governor was called out of town. I was disappointed."

"I'll bet you were. Oh, by the way, Bill," my friend was having trouble keeping a straight face, "the governor's first tax bill came up while you were downstairs. It passed, of course. And a reporter from the *Macon News* was just over inquiring why you weren't here to vote against it."

That was my first lesson in the hard-knock school of practical politics. I was to learn many others.

Shortly thereafter I took on Governor Sanders again—this time through his pride and joy, the Commission for Economy and Efficiency in Government, which Sanders himself had established. Chairman of the Commission was tall, gray, pipe-smoking William Bowdoin, who, if he hadn't already been one, would have had to become a distinguished Atlanta banker. He was perfect for the part.

I had received information that the Commission was abusing its authority and misspending the funds it had been given to probe the various departments of state government.

"If the Commission is worth anything," I argued, in one of my first speeches on the floor of the House, "then why isn't it saving the state some money? If it's really promoting efficiency, why must the governor ask the already overtaxed citizens of Georgia to dig further into their pockets? I submit that the state would be just as well off—probably better off—without this so-called economy and efficiency commission. And I tell you here and now, I intend to introduce a bill to abolish the Bowdoin Commission."

I was well pleased with the speech and with the response from my fellow representatives. But that night, while in my room at the Grady Hotel, I received a phone call from a North Georgia representative who had spent two decades in the House and was one of its most respected members. "Bill, I want to tell you something you're not going to like," he said. "You're wrong about the Bowdoin Commission. Dead wrong."

"What are you talking about?" I said. "Listen, I've got facts to back up everything I said." I had cited specific instances and amounts of wasteful spending by the Commission in my speech.

"Bill, your facts are wrong. That's what I called to tell you. You know I think a lot of you, Bill, and I think you should know the truth about this thing. You got your information from George L., right?"

"That's right. How did you know?" The former speaker, crafty old George L. Smith, had summoned me to his room the night before and spelled out the charges against the commission. He'd told me I was free to use the information any way I chose.

"George L. has been telling other legislators the same thing," my friend told me. "He's looking for a robot to go out and do his dirty work for him. I hate to have to tell you this, Bill, but he's using you in a personal vendetta against the Commission. There's something in state government he doesn't want found out, and he's trying to head off the Commission before that happens. Don't take my word—check the facts for yourself, then see if you still think George L. told you the truth."

That made sense. I skipped supper, and with a growing sense of depression, pulled the voluminous reports of the Bowdoin Commission from my desk drawer and belatedly began reading them page by page.

Next morning I was waiting at the door when the State Treasurer's office opened. I spent an hour before the House convened studying records of the Commission's spending.

By the time the Speaker banged his gavel to open the day's proceedings, I knew what I had to do.

The House Appropriations Committee had called

Bowdoin to appear before it that morning to answer my charges. Bowdoin sat now, puffing on his pipe, at the witness table. George L. leaned over to me and whispered, "Okay, killer, let's see what kind of guts you've got—go get 'im."

I'd already decided that there was only one way to square myself with a man of Bowdoin's character. I stood before the House and publicly apologized to him. I told him I had spoken too soon; that my charges had been made on the basis of erroneous information—information I should have checked first.

"I'm going to be a man," I told him. "I should have talked to you before I popped off like that."

Bowdoin, gentleman that he was, accepted the apology.

"You're a stout fellow, Mr. Laite," he told me.

I could feel George L.'s eyes boring into me.

The incident attracted a lot of publicity, little of it favorable to me. However, I felt I had done the right thing.

That first year in the legislature, I also chalked off a few "ups" to balance the "downs." My most satisfying success was my sponsorship of a gun control bill.

The Bibb County Grand Jury, after an investigation of the rising incidence of juvenile crime in the county, asked me to introduce the measure. It provided for the licensing of dealers in firearms fifteen inches or less in length, required the dealers to obtain a $25 license and file a $1,000 bond, and called for the revocation of the dealers' licenses if they sold handguns to juveniles.

I had no idea just now controversial the bill might be until I told another Bibb legislator, Rep. Denmark Groover, of my plans for introducing it.

"Hell, Bill," Groover told me, "the grand jury tried to get every other member of the Bibb delegation, me included, to introduce that thing. We wouldn't touch it." He shook his head. "When you start messing with people's guns, you're asking for trouble."

I respected his advice. He had been in and out of the Legislature for a long time. At one time Groover had been former Gov. Marvin Griffin's floor leader. Groover knew more about parliamentary procedure and behind-the-scenes politics than any man in the General Assembly, and he had passed a lot of it on to me during my first few weeks in the House.

"Well, you go ahead and introduce the damn thing— then just let it die in committee," Groover suggested. "That'll get you off the hook."

I shook my head. "No. I'm determined to push it through."

"All right, Bill, go ahead. But I put you on notice now, I'm going to have to fight you on it."

"Fair enough," I told him.

This was in 1963, before the national debate over gun control legislation had heated up. But I was soon to learn the difficulty of promoting a rational discussion of any measure having to do with guns. Opponents of my bill wasted no time in blasting it and me, invariably misinterpreting its purpose.

"Laite Explains Bill to Curb Pistol Sales," the headline read. And next day: *"Laite Again Explains Firearms Bill."* Then two days later: *"Laite Explains Gun Bill—Again and Again!"*

The latest story began, *"Rep. William E. Laite, Jr., said today his bill to license dealers in pistols—aimed at curbing illegal sales to minors—continues to be misinterpreted by hundreds."*

But while the public controversy raged on, I was working in private. I carried a copy of the bill in my pocket at all times, constantly "explaining" it to my fellow representatives in general terms and gathering in commitments for their support. It was a method of operation I had learned early and well from Denmark Groover.

Never, of course, would I misconstrue the bill—but somehow or other, most of the men who promised to support it had gotten the idea that it was directed only at black men.

I soon gathered more than enough commitments to insure passage in the House. But the bill had become snagged in committee—dead end for more than one good bill. It had been assigned, rightly enough, to the Judiciary Committee, and a member of that committee, my friend and mentor Mr. Groover, had a stranglehold on it there. It appeared the House would never even get a chance to vote on it.

But Groover had taught me well. One Friday afternoon, when there was barely a quorum on the floor, I rose and asked unanimous consent to have the bill withdrawn from Judiciary and placed in the Ways and Means Committee—of which I happened to be a member. Groover was absent from the Assembly, and there was no objection raised to my request.

The Ways and Means Committee quickly cleared the bill for House action—although one member with a puzzled frown said he would be curious to know "exactly what in the world a firearms bill has to do with Ways and Means," a committee that normally handles only money bills.

"That's easy," a friendly committee member answered. "It keeps robbers from taking money out of our banks."

I made sure the bill came up for a vote while Groover was attending to some business in the Senate. My commitments stood firm and it carried easily.

"That's all right, Bill," Groover told me when he found out later. "You slipped it through the House, but it will never get through the Senate."

The next week I prevailed upon Lt. Gov. Peter Zack Geer to call the bill up for a vote immediately after lunch on Wednesday. By then the National Rifle Association had marshaled its forces for a strong attack on the measure. I spent the whole lunch hour in the deserted Senate. As the senators left for lunch, pages began distributing material, all of it stamped with the NRA's return address, around the senators' desks. As soon as the pages left, I made the same rounds, collecting the material to be tucked away in my desk in the House.

The bill was called for Senate vote and passed with hardly a whisper against it.

Afterward I gave the NRA material back to the pages to be redistributed among the senators. I watched from the balcony as they began opening it, their eyes widening as they saw the NRA's long list of reasons why the bill should be defeated.

On July 1, 1963, Gov. Sanders signed the bill into law. The *Macon News* saw fit to comment editorially: *"Through national efforts by Senator* (Thomas J.) *Dodd, and local efforts by men such as Rep. Laite, some lives will surely be saved by keeping guns out of the hands of the irresponsible and by licensing sellers of weapons to underline their responsibilities."*

The bill and the resulting law remained controversial, though, until that day in Dallas, in November, 1963. Then, overnight, I became a hero.

7

MY SECOND YEAR at the Capitol in 1964 was an ideal period for any serious student of the political arts. I was still learning more about practical politics every day on the job.

Some of the most important pieces of legislation that had been considered in many years came before that session. Arm-twisting and wheeling-and-dealing of every conceivable nature were commonplace practice.

Gov. Carl Sanders was a hard-shell pragmatist, with a slight Machiavellian touch, a man who knew that politics was simply the art of the possible. But there were times when, even if a thing weren't possible, he somehow found a way to make it possible. The only bills Carl Sanders failed to push through the legislature, by one means or another, were the ones he didn't introduce.

Sanders was smart enough to steer clear of the mixed drink bill, though. He knew he couldn't afford to be tainted by backing that one. At the same time, he wanted to avoid making the powerful enemies he would have made by actively opposing it.

Sander's hand-picked Speaker of the House could be a pretty slippery fish, too, when the occasion demanded. George T. Smith (called George T. to distinguish him from former Speaker George L. Smith) couldn't manage to stay quite so neutral as the governor; being a self-styled churchman, a believer in clean living, no smoking and no drinking, it was naturally expected that he would oppose any pro-drink measure. And, for the record, he did so. However, on the afternoon when the hot-potato bill came up for a vote in the House, the Speaker was mysteriously missing.

Then, as the time for the crucial vote neared, House aides began moving around the chamber pulling the long, red velvet draperies over the windows that led to anterooms on both sides. One of the aides came around, whispering to us in a low voice, "It's going to be a hand vote."

A vote by show of hands, of course, was not officially recorded. You could tell the preachers back home that you'd done all you could, but they'd passed the "dang thing" in spite of you, and no one would ever know the difference. This had happened on other controversial votes. Routine bills, on the other hand, were decided by pulling a switch at your desk—which flashed a "yea" or "nay" vote in red or green lights alongside your name; and at the same time your vote was recorded for posterity on print-outs.

The Speaker Pro Tem rather nervously called for a show of hands and, sure enough, a wide majority of the hands present shot into the air.

But just then, a wily photographer for the *Atlanta Constitution,* his camera equipped with a wide-angle lens, came out of nowhere, darted down in front and snapped a picture, then slipped quickly out a side entrance.

There were a lot of chagrined representatives the next morning when the newspaper hit the streets. The picture was spread across seven columns, and the face of almost every man who had voted for the mixed drink bill was right there for all to see.

+ + +

Congressional reapportionment took up most of the session, though, and caused more heated debate than any other measure.

The Supreme Court had ruled that Georgia's ten districts were out of proportion in terms of population, and they would have to be redrawn. This would seem, on the surface, to be a largely mathematical chore, a mere matter of maps and population-density charts; and that's all it was—until politics came into the equation.

The major problem, politically speaking, was to redraw the congressional districts without doing too much harm to any incumbent's reelection prospects. That spelled bad news for our Sixth District. The venerable Carl Vinson was retiring after fifty distinguished years of service in the U.S. House. Therefore, most of the state's representatives wanted to do virtually all the carving in his old Sixth District, leaving the other nine districts reasonably intact and their nine congressmen mollified.

But every representative seemed to have his own idea of how this could best be done. Every time you turned around somebody was spreading a different map of Georgia under your nose with a maze of lines slicing up the state into jigsawed districts that suited his own interests.

Next to Macon, the most maligned area in the state in the redistricting proposals was the capital city, Atlanta. The rural legislators had never lost a great deal of love for the metropolis—although they were more than willing to share in its night life each year when they came into town for the sessions.

One South Georgia representative offered—quite seriously, he insisted—his so-called "Pie Plan" for reapportionment. Starting dead-center of downtown Atlanta, he neatly divided the state into ten pie-wedge slices. "That way," he explained, straightfaced, "everybody gets a little bit of the place."

Most of the discussion on the issue, though, was dead serious, and as it went on and on, week after week, with still no agreement in sight, tempers began to wear thin. Sanders felt that his prestige would suffer if the Legislature didn't comply with the court's mandate and come up with a workable plan by the close of the forty-day session. He began applying pressure.

As the session drew toward its final days, many of the representatives were no longer even on speaking terms with one another. In an effort to smooth a few ruffled feathers, calm some stormy seas, and perhaps get the House in a better mood to settle the issue, I took the floor one morning on a point of personal privilege.

"Mr. Speaker and Gentlemen of the House," I began. "Like everyone else, I've done a good deal of research on this matter, and I have discovered two important facts.

"One is that there are 205 separate redistricting plans in the hearts of the members of this House. And the second indisputable fact is that only one congressional redistricting plan can be put into effect.

"Like every other legislator in the chamber, I have my own little redistricting program . . . called the 'Better Laite Than Never' plan or, for short, the 'Laite Plan.' . . . It is all things to all men. It pays tribute to the associations of the past and looks forward to the population growths of the future. It keeps any incumbent congressman from having to run against another, yet opens things up for any of you, or anyone else, who wants to run.

"It takes care of the largest cities . . . and it protects rural areas. . . . It takes the four million-plus people of Georgia and divides them into ten districts of exactly equal population. The 'Better Laite Than Never' plan will be welcomed by the farmers, the city slickers, the rich, the poor, the wets, the drys, the billboard people, the anti-billboard people, by beauticians, osteopaths and tax collectors. . . . It keeps the fall-line citizens walking a straight line, yet gets us all out of the woods.

"The 'Better Laite Than Never' plan . . . would help Georgians who so desire to quit smoking and at the same time assure those who like to smoke that they would continue to enjoy that rich, full flavor. It would rejuvenate tired blood, eliminate dental cavities, cure alcoholism, slow down reckless drivers, abolish diaper rash, and make every legislative proposal understandable to every legislator.

"Of course, by now every member of this body knows that the 'Better Laite Than Never' plan is only a dream—a dream that is dear to each of us. . . . But each man's dream is different, unfortunately. The point of my remarks is plain. We cannot each have his own way . . . and ignore others."

+   +   +

The last day of the session came, and still no agreement had been reached. The House had passed one plan, the Senate another, and there seemed to be little possibility of their reconciling the differences.

Sanders was really tightening the screws as the last night wore one, but still it appeared almost certain that a compromise would not be worked out before midnight, when the session officially was supposed to close. All eyes were on the official clock, set on the balcony level, just below the rail. The House was a madhouse. All night long members had been leaving the floor for extended visits to the men's room, returning after each foray a little more red-faced and loud-mouthed than before. Almost continually the Speaker's gavel was pounding for order.

Then shortly before midnight, a custodial officer leaned over the balcony rail and stopped the clock. The minute hand stayed there, locked just short of "12," as the final action on reapportionment unfolded in the midst of bedlam.

The sponsor of the House bill had sold out under pressure from the governor. He was not even in the chamber when the final vote on the Senate bill, backed by Sanders, was taken. By a narrow margin, it passed, and for all intents and purposes the issue was settled.

But some of the members weren't ready to go home yet—they wanted to get in their final licks, including some pithy comments on their opinion of the way the Senate bill had been rammed through. No one was better qualified for this than short, squat "Sloppy" Floyd, a notoriously independent legislator from the hills of North Georgia. Finally, Floyd succeeded in getting the Speaker's permission to address the House. He began spouting forth some of the most fiery rhetoric heard in those chambers for a long time. But the Speaker was anxious to end the pandemonium and adjourn the session. He signaled the custodian to restart the clock. When the hands finally touched midnight, the Speaker and the

Lieutenant Governor, presiding over the Senate, would look at each other through the open doors of the two chambers and bring their gavels down simultaneously, adjourning the General Assembly for the year.

Groover and I were watching as the custodian started the clock going again. "Why, that rotten little— He's not even going to let Sloppy finish!" Groover yelled. He took off in a dead run. When I spotted him, seconds later, he was leaning over the balcony railing, reaching for the clock. I watched in fascination the clock's long, tumbling fall, saw it shatter into a hundred pieces across the floor of the House.

The red-faced Speaker would delay no longer. He raised his voice above the din—"I declare this house adjourned!"—he banged his gavel down, with a sound like a pistol shot, turned, and hurriedly left the floor.

Observers in the gallery, meantime, were heaping verbal abuse on the House members as they began straggling out. The Georgia Sweet Potato Association had placed a small bag of its product on each representative's desk earlier in the day—now some members were ripping open the bags and firing potatoes up into the gallery.

I popped one guy a good one, right between the shoulder blades, as he turned and ran for cover.

8

THAT THIRD NIGHT, there in the Tarrant County Jail, I did a lot of thinking about our son, Bill. It was the second anniversary of the day he had died.

He was our first-born, a chubby baby, with my cheeks and Marilyn's eyes, who grew up to be an intelligent, well-mannered boy. While I was in the State Legislature, he delighted in going along with me to Atlanta at least once during each session to serve as a page on the floor. He could carry more soft drinks on a trip than any other page there, and his great enthusiasm made him a favorite there.

On the morning after the federal grand jury indicted me, Bill had walked into the bathroom where I was shaving. "Daddy," he asked me, "what does 'indictment' mean?" He had the morning paper in his hands. Spread across the front page of the *Macon Telegraph* was the bold headline: *"Rep. Laite Faces 2 Indictments by Dallas Jury."*

I had no answer for him.

That was the only time I ever felt real anger toward the federal officials responsible for my case. If there had been an FHA man in the room at that moment I might have strangled him with my bare hands—not for what they were doing to me, but for what they were doing to my family.

The indictment served one worthwhile purpose, though. It gave me more time to spend with my son. The shadow of the charges cut into the business, and for days at a time I had little or nothing to do. Little Bill loved to fish more than anything else, and the two of us began going fishing every day, if only for a few minutes.

Soon after that, the Senate Democratic Caucus was meeting in Atlanta. I'd planned to take Bill along with us, but he didn't want to miss school.

After we'd finished, I picked up Marilyn at the hotel to drive back to Macon. She told me she had just called home and that Little Bill had gone fishing with one of his friends at High Falls.

I grinned at her. "Hey, that's great."

Driving through Jackson, near High Falls, we passed the local hospital and noticed a good many police and sheriff's cars parked outside.

When we got home we found several cars parked in

front of our house. "Bill—something's wrong!" Marilyn had the door open before I brought the car to a stop.

We went in by the side door, and I almost bumped into a neighbor. He put a hand on my shoulder. "Bill, I swear, it looks like every time I see you lately something bad has happened."

I grabbed the front of his coat. "What are you talking about? What's happened?"

"You mean you don't know? God—oh, God, I can't tell you." He turned away. Marilyn was almost in hysterics. Another neighbor came running over. He'd overheard.

"Bill, your son's dead," he said. "He drowned at High Falls."

I drew back my fist to hit him. "You're lying!" I screamed. "He *couldn't* have drowned! He could swim like a fish—he could swim better than I could!"

Marilyn had fainted. Then other neighbors began swarming in, having seen our car outside.

The story got through to me in pieces. Bill and a friend had been fishing from a rock at the head of the falls. My son had picked up a stick, a piece of driftwood, and asked his pal if he wanted it. When the boy said no, Little Bill had tried to throw it in the water, to watch it go over the falls—and somehow he'd lost his balance and fallen fifty feet to the bottom of the falls.

I was right about one thing. He hadn't drowned. We later found out that he had hit the rocks just beneath the water when he fell.

The next day I went up there, just to look at the site for myself. I found his reel and bait still on the rocks where he had left them.

I stood on the spot where he had lost his footing and remembered that he had been wearing a pair of brand new nonskid boots.

He had died fourteen days before his thirteenth birthday.

That black anniversary night, remembering, I prayed and wept, there in my cell in the Tarrant County Jail.

9

THE NEXT MORNING, the beginning of my fourth day behind bars, I was up at the first clanging of the bell.

The day before, I had finally struck up a conversation with one of my fellow inmates. David, who seemed to be the most likable of the bunch, had slouched down on the floor beside me and asked if I knew anything about the law.

"Why do you ask?" I responded.

He told me about his case. He'd been arrested for trying to pass bad checks. The police in the little Texas town had kept him in jail for three days without letting him contact a lawyer or anyone else. "I mean, isn't that illegal?" he asked me. "Don't they have to let you call your lawyer in the first twenty-four hours?"

I told him I wasn't sure, but I thought he was right. I added: "It's not unusual at all for a sheriff or a police chief in a small town to interpret the law in any way he chooses. You're lucky they didn't beat hell out of you for good measure."

"Oh, they did that, too," he said, smiling.

That seemed to break the ice, and he proceeded to complain to me about all the bad breaks he'd had in his lifetime. He said he'd bounced from job to job ever since he'd gotten out of the Navy three years earlier. The bad check arrest had been his third on the same charge, and the judge had dealt him a stiff three-year penalty.

He was a nice-looking guy, about twenty-three, and he seemed intelligent and well educated. He told me he had gone no further than the tenth grade but had taken correspondence courses while in the Navy, acquiring the equivalent of a high school diploma.

He seemed to enjoy talking to me. Probably he was glad to find someone who would carry on a normal conversation with him. I was entertaining hope of gaining an ally. Two against four would be better odds than one against five. (I couldn't place Danny on either side, in his condition.)

David began telling me, on his own initiative, about the others in the dayroom, all of whom were either napping or talking among themselves so that there was no danger of them overhearing what we were saying.

Mike—the self-appointed "tank boss"—was of Mexican ancestry. He'd been in and out of reformatories since he was a small kid. Now twenty-three, he'd been involved in a variety of adult crimes, and was currently serving a twelve-year sentence for auto theft. He was about my height—around five feet, ten inches—but must have weighed at least 220 to my 180, and most of the difference was muscle, not fat.

Mike's right-hand man, who did a lot of his dirty work for him, was Charlie—about twenty-seven, blond, blunt-nosed, with a broad, scarred face. He was only about five-five but was very brash and aggressive. David said Charlie had been in prison a good part of his life. Like Mike, he was serving a twelve-year term; in his case, it was for aggravated assault, which didn't surprise me at all. I had once heard Charlie talking about another guy who stole a girl from him. "When I get out of here I'm going to show that runt how it feels to be broke in half," he'd sneered.

Gary, twenty-three, son of a Methodist minister, had been convicted of raping the wife of a detective in Fort Worth. He was awaiting a decision from the Texas Supreme Court on his appeal of his life sentence. Tall and slim, he was extremely quiet and easygoing. He had only two tattoos, far fewer than most of the others.

Richard was about twenty-one. He had a narrow face with a long nose that bent oddly to one side. He had bushy black hair and brows, conniving eyes, and a thin mouth that seemed to be locked in a permanent sneer. He was awaiting trial for cold-bloodedly shooting a taxi driver to death in Indianapolis, and if I had been on his jury, I'd have been tempted to vote guilty on the basis of how he looked, if for no other reason.

The quiet black man's name was Raymond. He was pitch black, tall—three or four inches over six feet—and built like the tight end for the Baltimore Colts. David told me he was serving four years for armed robbery. I guessed him to be no more than nineteen or twenty.

Our conversation—during which I had almost forgotten to feel sorry for myself—ended abruptly when the mailman came around. Mike snapped at David, "Get off your ass and bring me that mail!" David hustled to obey.

I began tensing up. I felt reasonably sure there would be another letter for me.

There were, in fact, two. Mike held them aloft, high above his head, for everyone to see. I could make out Marilyn's handwriting on one of them. Mike jammed it into his pocket without opening it.

The other letter, in a larger envelope, he unfolded after ripping off the envelope.

He was in an unusually nasty mood, even for him.

"Now what the hell is this stuff?" The contents seemed to set him in a rage. "What in the hell . . . is this a bunch of religious crap?"

I knew immediately what it was. It had to be material from my mother. A devout Christian, she had promised to send me daily devotionals to study while I was in prison. Once the *Valdosta Times* had interviewed her for an article entitled "What My Church Means to Me." It had taken her thirty paragraphs to give a still incomplete answer to the question.

I was enraged by Mike's ridiculing the material she had sent me. It was all I could do to make myself stand still. I was hoping he was finished.

He wasn't.

He threw the letter and other material to the floor, stomping them underfoot. "If there's one thing I can't stand," he roared, "it's a lot of Jesus junk!"

I couldn't bluff or delay any longer. The fury rushing up inside me, I moved toward him. "All right," I said, "that's enough!"

He looked at me, his jaw sagging in surprise. Then he grinned and glanced at Charlie. "Well, it looks like we're gonna have to take the dude, don't it?"

I saw Richard and Gary move to back up the other two.

Things happened fast then. I was grappling with Charlie, who had stepped between Mike and me, when I saw a blur of movement, heard shouts—and the next thing I knew both Mike and Richard were on the floor.

It was Raymond. The lanky Negro must have covered the distance from the commode in three long strides and decked the two men simultaneously, apparently with very little trouble.

Then, almost casually, he wrapped a powerful black arm around Charlie's throat and peeled him off me.

"All right now, that's it!" He said it softly, but they all heard him and they all froze right where they were—Mike and Richard still flat on their backs on the floor, Gary locked in the middle of a stride in my direction.

David, I saw with satisfaction, had kept his seat on one of the benches. Danny lay against the wall, watching it all, his chin on his fist.

I was glad that my mental dividing up of the sides had put Raymond on the wrong team.

"Now, if you want some of this man here, you're gonna have to go through me to get it," Raymond told them, pointing a long finger at first one, then another of them, Charlie still in his grasp and working with his hands to loosen the arm around his neck.

For several seconds no one moved; the only sound was the rasping of Charlie trying to draw in some air.

Finally Mike broke the silence. "Aw, hell . . . the dude's not worth it." He hadn't moved from his place on the floor; now he rolled onto his side, turning his back on the rest of us.

Slowly the other men drifted back to their places. Raymond let go of Charlie, who walked away shakily after almost falling to the floor, rubbing his throat, mumbling something incoherent under his breath.

I grabbed the mail from my mother and then, in a flash of bravado, reached over and snatched Marilyn's letter from Mike's pocket. He never even looked up at me.

Without another word, Raymond turned and went back to his seat on the toilet.

+   +   +

Raymond's cell was next to mine. Later that night, I reached through my bars and tapped on his. I didn't hear him move, but I could hear his breathing and knew he had come to the front of his cell. Only the wall between the two units separated us.

"Why did you help me?" I asked. It was the first time I'd spoken a word to him.

"You're from Macon, Georgia, right?"

"Yeah."

"That's where Otis Redding and James Brown are from, isn't it?"

"That's right."

"That's reason enough," he said.

After Raymond interceded for me, the tension in the jail relaxed somewhat; but the relief was a relative thing. I still felt, every minute of the say, that my life and safety were in danger.

Mike was still needling me off and on, joined from time to time by Charlie. They seemed to be trying to push me as far as they could without getting Raymond involved.

The first time we were out of Raymond's hearing range, Charlie whispered to me across a distance of several feet: "Just wait, dude. The nigger'll be getting out of here any day now. What'll you do then?"

I wondered if he was right. The days kept crawling by and still there was no indication when I would be transferred to a permanent prison. I was growing more and more desperate.

Every day was a succession of crises. I never knew when I might be forced into another showdown situation. At the same time, I wondered how much worse physical punishment could be than this perpetual battle of nerves.

+   +   +

I grew to love my little cell. It was barely three feet wide, with just enough room to stand between the bunk and the wall. But inside, once the steel door slammed shut, I could relax, knowing I was safe; knowing they couldn't get me. I dreaded the mornings and returning to the dayroom.

The first night I thought, as the closing door secured me in my cell, I could anticipate a little silence and tranquility. No such thing. The yelling and cursing continued and seemed to escalate when there was no possibility of actually carrying out the threats. Two or three of the men would yell back and forth between cells, uttering the vilest of threats, each describing in precise detail exactly what he would do to the other if he could reach him; the other blaring back his version of what mayhem he would loose on the other as soon as they returned to the dayroom.

I tremulously imagined the bloodbath that would take place the next morning when they could finally get at each other's throats. As it turned out, the first thing they all did when they entered the dayroom the next morning was to lie down on the floor and go back to sleep. After a couple of nights it became clear that the nighttime word battle was a mere ritual, as much a part of the settling-down-for-the-night routine of some of the prisoners as reading a magazine or the newspaper in bed had been for me at home.

The cursing and threatening continued every night, sometimes for an hour or longer. Finally, everyone would drift off to sleep.

Each time I entered my individual cell was a moment of relief for me. I had two or three devotionals my mother had sent me. I kept them in my cell to avoid more confrontations. On many occasions, after the others had finally gone to sleep, I would read some of these inspirational thoughts, in the glare of the never-extinguished lights, and then I would kneel on the hard floor alongside my bunk and quietly ask God to provide me with enough strength and courage to get through the next day, to accept things as they were, and not to lapse into self-pity and longing for what was not and could not be.

Many times I felt that I just couldn't take it anymore. I felt that the seams were about to burst, and I would come completely unraveled if I didn't get some help. I would curse myself for being weak but it didn't help. I wanted to get out of prison so badly, depression would grow and grow inside me. In the waning hours of the night, I would lie wide-eyed on my bunk or stand in the finally-silent building, my hands and face against the cool steel bars of the cell door, and the utter helplessness of my predicament would seep through me, penetrating every part of me.

I could imagine spending my whole year-and-a-day term in that jail in this completely helpless state. They had me where they wanted me; they could do anything with me they desired. I was in a state of involuntary servitude. I had no recourse; I couldn't telephone anybody or write anybody without the letter being censored. They had locked me up and thrown away the key.

It was at times like this, when the depression was worst, that prayer seemed to provide me with a new strength, enough to carry on awhile longer.

+ + +

The bell woke the jail's inhabitants at 5:00 each morning. Noise pollution in the outside world is nothing compared to that in the Tarrant County Jail. The shrill sound of the bell bounced deafeningly off the metallic walls and ceilings. I learned to anticipate it, and I would jam my fingers into my ears. At 9:00 each night the bell would ring again to flush us out of the dayroom and back to our cells. In between there was the constant banging of steel doors, the amplified blare of the guards' voices over the loudspeakers, and the screaming and cursing of prisoners in my tank and others on the seventh floor.

As soon as we were out of bed each morning, a mop and broom would be passed from cell to cell so that each man could clean up his area. Each prisoner would reach his hand through the bars, straining toward the next cell to reach the broom and mop being thrust his way.

One of the few positive things about the other inmates that impressed me was the efficient manner in which they went about mopping and sweeping their cells and the hallway when it was their turn. I don't know if they tackled the job with such vigor in order to work off excess energy, if they just wanted to keep things clean, or if they feared an inspection and possible discipline. But I never saw anything resembling an inspection while I was there.

After we finished cleaning up our cells, the doors would slide open and we'd head for the dayroom.

Each tank consisted of a dayroom, dividing hall, and eight or more individual cells. I was told that there were about 140 prisoners on the seventh floor.

Mealtimes were degrading experiences. The food was miserable. The usual menu was lima beans, spinach, and turnips. The rule was that no food could be returned; what wasn't eaten must be flushed down the toilet. This was apparently so that the jail officials could boast that "the food must be good, because it's all eaten."

I made a lot of trips to the toilet.

Breakfast was usually one piece of scorched toast and a cup of lousy coffee, but once we did get syrup on the toast. Once, too, we were given cereal, but it had all been mixed together in a master pot and was hopelessly soupy by the time it got to us. On the rare occasions other than breakfast when we got bread, it was always soggy from contact with the other food.

The food, on tin pans resembling dog trays, was passed through the knee-level slot in the wall by trusties. If you weren't ready to grab it, they dropped it on the floor. You stuck your cup through the slot to be filled with coffee or tea. Sometimes—I never knew whether by error or intent—hot coffee would be poured on your wrist instead of in your cup. Sometimes, too, a trusty would break up the monotony of his day by urinating in your cup or on your arm.

It became a game to watch the other prisoners stick their hand and cup through the hole and then, clenching their teeth, hold the cup there until they heard and felt the liquid pour in, then draw it quickly back into the dayroom. It was fun—until it came your turn. Then you had to weigh your thirst against what might happen to your hand.

I lost about ten pounds while I was there. Eventually I began giving most of my food to David or Danny.

I learned that drinking hot water helps kill appetite. Even so, I stayed hungry most of the time. At mealtime I'd have made up my mind that I could eat whatever they brought, but one look at the food would destroy any inclination to eat.

+   +   +

I finally gained Danny's confidence enough so that he would talk to me. He said he'd been arrested for stealing money out of a cigarette machine at a service station. His sister, a waitress, was the only living member of his immediate family. Danny was the only person in the tank whom I ever heard express any remorse for his crime. He talked about the possibility of getting into college when he got out of jail. His sister, he said, had promised to help pay his tuition.

He never mentioned his assault; neither did anyone else in the tank.

Danny never said a word to any of the other men, not even David, who made an effort to be friendly to him. Charlie and Mike would badger him occasionally, and he would merely drop his head and stare silently at the floor.

Thinking back, I tried to recall whether David had taken part in Danny's attack. I hoped he hadn't, but I couldn't remember for sure. All the men had been new to me then, and I couldn't distinguish between them yet. I knew it had been Mike who knocked him unconscious with a sock stuffed with soap, and I recalled seeing Raymond on the toilet just after it was all over. But the other attackers remained a blur in my mind.

Danny still limped sadly every time he had to go to

the meal slot, the commode, or back and forth to his cell.

The veteran prisoners had something going all the time, anything to relieve the boredom. I was reminded of trips to the zoo, watching the monkeys squatting in their cages, intently picking fleas off each other.

Several of the men—Gary, the quiet one, was the best at this—had learned to swing-jump across the bars of the dayroom, quickly traversing the distance from one end to the other without ever touching the floor.

When they weren't sleeping, they spent much of their time gambling, for money or cigarettes. The gambling led to numerous fights. They usually wrapped washcloths around their fists, so as not to leave marks on either their hands or their opponent's face and body. But frequently one of them would fall against the bars or metal table or bench and suffer some cuts and bruises.

Charlie started the majority of the scraps. Although Mike was the "boss," Charlie did most of the fighting. Often without provocation, he would walk up to a fellow inmate and lay him out on the floor with one or two savage punches.

He often assisted Mike in the daily battle of nerves when the mail arrived.

"Go get me the mail, Charlie," Mike would say.

Charlie would be on his feet before Mike finished the sentence, anticipating some fun. After he took the mail from the slot, Charlie would strut slowly around the tank, holding the letters in his hands, flashing them under the noses of the rest of us too fast for anyone to see if his name was on an envelope.

Then, after he tired of this, Charlie would deliver the mail to Mike.

Some of the letters Mike would read aloud, savoring the intimate passages with lip-smacking pleasure. The letter's rightful recipient would sit in the throes of helpless anger and humiliation while the others laughed at him.

Sooner or later all the laughers, with the exception of Charlie, were on the receiving end of Mike's taunts. Raymond neither received mail nor took part in the razzing of those whose letters were sidetracked by Charlie and Mike.

Sometimes Mike, after reading a letter from one of the men's wives or girlfriends, would take a pencil and paper in hand and loudly compose his own reply.

There was one from Richard's wife. Mike read a particularly erotic part aloud, in which she expressed her bodily desires vividly. Then he began to write:

"My Darling Sarah,

"Richard has just shown me your last letter. Since I'll be out before him, and since he don't want you to keep on going without any loving, he has told me it's OK with him if I come to see you.

"Is that all right with you, Sarah? I promise you, you won't be disappointed. Fact is, after one night with me, you'll forget ole Richard's even alive.

"Here is what I'm going to do to you. . . ."

Richard sat seething, trembling, and I wondered how

a man who was supposed to be a coldblooded murderer could sit there like that.

I have no idea whether or not Mike ever mailed the letter. He might as well have, though, because the others certainly thought he did.

Sometimes Mike would keep a letter for days, often until the owner found a way to bribe him out of it. Sometimes he made them beg. None of the others ever remotely hinted that he might challenge Mike's authority. I assumed that Mike had established his physical supremacy in previous battles, although David couldn't recall him ever being in a one-on-one fight.

"It's always been him and one or two against a lone victim," David said. "I've never even thought of trying to take him," he went on, after I raised the question. "But Charlie—or even Richard. Now that might be a fight worth the price of a ticket.

After the incident with Raymond, Mike never opened any of my mail again, but he sometimes kept my letters in his pocket for hours or days at a time before finally tossing them at my feet.

Once or twice I almost got irritated enough to try to take them away from him. Then I would weigh my chances and talk myself out of it.

+   +   +

David and I were sitting side by side against the day-room wall. Charlie had been to the commode and was walking back past us. Charlie leaned over, smiling, as if to ask a question, and struck David on the temple with his fist. David crumpled over as if he was dead.

I sprang to my feet, wondering if I were next. Charlie walked on by. As I helped David back into a sitting position and he shook the stars out of his head, Charlie muttered something to Mike about "a few more around here" getting the same treatment. "I'm going to have to whip some more of them into line," he said, looking directly at me.

The tension seemed to build up between us as the day wore on. The time for the noon meal came, and Charlie seemed to forget me. He and Gary got into a shoving match for a place at the food window, and they growled at each other the rest of the day.

I was always last in line to get fed. For one thing, I was in no hurry to eat that slop; for another, I didn't want to get into a pushing contest for a place in line. There was only room for four men to sit and eat at the table. A couple of times, when a space would be left I would start to sit down. Each time, just as I'd get one leg inside the bench, Charlie or Mike would push in, shoving me away with, "Hell, no, dude, that's my place," even though they'd already begun eating somewhere else. From then on I ate on the floor, setting the pan between my knees.

After a meal, Charlie liked to spin his tin plate across the room like a Frisbee, sending it clattering off the wall near someone's head.

A choice spot during the long hours of the day was

underneath the table. This was the only place in the day-room where a sleeper could escape the glare of the lights that burned all the time. Charlie, Mike, and Richard gathered under there one day, their legs sticking out in three directions, and I could overhear enough of the mumbling to know that they were plotting something. I moved as inconspicuously as possible to the end of the room near Raymond and sat with my back in a corner.

It was the day for exchanging dirty laundry for clean. The swap was made in the dayroom, and each person was given clean clothing and towels. In a few minutes, Mike, Charlie, and Richard got to their feet, moving in my direction with towels in hand. They veered at the last minute and went to the shower, where they held the towels inside and turned on the water to get them sopping wet.

I thought I knew what was coming. I was relieved when they headed toward the other end of the dayroom instead of toward me.

Gary was their victim this time. He was often their ally, but these three had no compunctions about getting their kicks at the expense of a sometimes-pal.

Gary was asleep, lying on his stomach, clad only in his undershorts. Mike, Richard, and Charlie attacked him with the wet towels from three sides simultaneously, sending stinging, slingshot-like blows to his backside and legs with the ends of the towels. He arose howling, trying to cover himself with his hands, taking a lot of punishment on his arms and head, looking for somewhere to run. He finally darted between Richard and Mike and dove underneath the table as the welts began to rise on his body. He was crying from the pain and begging them to stop.

His three tormenters, screaming with laughter, threw their towels under to him, and he began applying the soothing wetness to his blistered body. Then Mike, Charlie, and Richard stretched out on the floor and went to sleep.

10

"KEEP YOUR CHIN UP. Before you know it, it'll all be behind you," people told me before I left Macon to begin serving my time.

They'll never know what a lie that was. Time passed with such agonizingly slowness first in the Tarrant County Jail and later in prison that I sometimes wondered if I would ever be free again.

How must those prisoners feel who serve terms of five, ten, or twenty years?

There was no way to know what time it was. After a few days in jail, I began using meals as a yardstick. My immediate goal would be the next one. After breakfast I'd look forward to lunch. After lunch I'd tell myself I had half the day behind me. After supper, my spirits would begin to rise, because I knew I had only three or four hours to go before we were placed back in our cells, and another day would be gone.

One of the things my mother sent me was a calendar with a devotion for each day. Someone said before I left home that the worst thing you could do in prison, psychologically, was to keep a calendar. It tended to make one more conscious of time, they said, and slowed down its passage. But I felt a certain satisfaction from reading the day's devotion in the relative privacy of my little cell, then crossing off the day on the calendar. It seemed to give me some initiative to keep plugging for one more day, and then still another.

I lived minute by minute. I didn't even try to project my thoughts ahead for much as one day. I was constantly matching wits with an antagonist, and never able to relax. My ability to parry verbal thrusts with my politician's tongue helped me smooth out a number of confrontations that could easily have developed into brawls.

At first it was difficult for me to look at the other prisoners eye-to-eye. They all presented such an aura of ferocity that I was overwhelmed. I finally learned to gaze at a spot directly between a man's eyebrows, and I was actually able to stare down more than one of them this way.

My time in the dayroom was divided between sitting on the floor, leaning against the wall, and sitting at the table. By the second day I was beginning to feel sore all over, and the soreness continued to increase the longer I was there.

There was nothing even slightly soft to sit on. In the dayroom, the choice was between metal benches and the concrete floor. Even in the cells at night there were no mattresses on the metal bunks. From time to time I would sit on one of the benches in the dayroom, with my upper body hunched forward, my lower body jutting far back, so that my weight was on the back part of my thighs. This gave my aching buttocks some relief.

I came to understand why Raymond had commandeered the commode to sit on. It was the best seat in the house.

I kept hoping against hope that I would get pulled out of this jail and be sent to another installation. Every time I heard footsteps coming down the hall, I held my breath, praying that someone would call "Laite" and tell me to come out. When a door clanged far down the hall, I began to plead with the Man Upstairs: "Let the hollow, ringing footsteps coming my way be those of a guard coming to get me!" A stroke of fate is going to get me out; I'd pray, maybe, this time, the guard will tell me it was all a mistake, I'm free to go home; I will go back to Macon, and they'll forget the whole, mixed up, affair.

On my fourth day in jail I wrote in my makeshift diary: "Breakfast was cold rolls and jelly. I ate a rare meal. Just doesn't look like I'll ever get out of this place."

A day later I wrote: "Confinement is really getting to me. The tension is constant. I feel like you could cut the air with a knife."

A couple of days later, I received a single short letter

from a young neighbor. He was a boy who had become close to me after my son's death. I scribbled in the diary: "Was very depressed and lonesome and disappointed; no other mail and no other news."

The few letters I was permitted to receive were read over and over again. Just rereading them gave me a spiritual lift, and reminded me that somebody cared, something I ached to know.

In a letter to Marilyn, I wrote, "I've just received your letter. It was a real joy, and it was all I could do to keep from showing emotion, it made me so happy." Getting mail in care of the Tarrant County Jail was depressing, though.

"I was hoping to be out of here by now," I wrote. "This confinement is so hard to get used to. Time moves so slowly. You cannot imagine the adjustment. I am thankful for you and my family."

Thoughts of my family were a major resource for me. Thinking of my wife and daughters, and even of my son who died, encouraged me to endure whatever came my way.

I promised myself I would make my time in prison fruitful, but as it turned out, my first concern in jail was staying alive and healthy, and my second concern was staying sane.

I finally gained sufficient control over my mind so that I could use it to help me accept some of the physical difficulties. I would imagine myself somewhere else—at home, usually, on a soft couch, my feet propped up, listening to a melody of soft music, Marilyn hovering lovingly over me, Jenny and Kelly nearby, perhaps a cool drink in my hand and another one already pressing gently and cooly against the inside walls of my stomach.

A booming curse or a clanging metal door, jarred me back to reality.

In jail you miss the little things, the little conveniences. I would glance at my wrist to see what time it was, and see nothing but my wrist. I would wish for a newspaper or a newscast to find out what was going on in the outside world. There were no books or newspapers to read, of course. One of the men had part of a Texas law book, which he read through and through.

I would think that it would mean so much to see a familiar face or hear a familiar voice. Then I would realize how horrified any of my friends or family would be to see me—dirty, stinking, ill-shaven, pale, wearing convict clothes.

What would I do if one of my political associates walked in. I could imagine myself introducing him to my "roommates":

"Carl, I'd like to have you meet Mike, here. Mike's a very fine sadist and an outstanding sexual pervert. He particularly likes to rape helpless boys, preferably when they're unconscious.

"And this is his friend, Charlie. Charlie is well known for his highly developed sense of brutality; he has made an art of bullying and torturing the rest of us here.

"And the naked one over there, playing with himself, is Richard. He's a real killer, Richard is . . ."

And so on.

I realized over and over, the longer I was there, that I had absolutely nothing in common with anyone else in the jail. All the conversation—the entire atmosphere—was filled with vulgarity, filth, despair. Even my attempts to talk with David usually ended with him pouring out his miseries to me, in the vain hope there might be something I could do to help him.

The overall effect of such a barrage was a steady tearing down of my defenses, a continual assault on my moral barriers, a gnawing and clawing at my fortifications of hope, serenity, and confidence.

I was bothered a great deal by a change that had come over me almost without my realizing it. I found myself using the same filthy language as the others. No matter how hard I fought against it, I seemed to be absorbing the lingo of the tank, as if by osmosis.

After Raymond had come to my aid, I talked with the tall Negro from time to time—or tried to. But he wasn't much of a conversationalist. He communicated mostly through grunts and shakes of his head. I did learn that he was a musician—a guitarist—and that he liked to write songs. He showed me one he had written, and I thought it was pretty good. I promised to help him get it published, but I left the jail without learning how to get in touch with him.

During my last few days in jail I spent a lot of my

time rolling cigarettes for David and Gary. I gradually got to know them better.

Gary, the Methodist minister's son, denied he had raped the detective's wife. He claimed she had seduced *him,* then yelled "rape" when they were discovered. Apparently they'd been caught red-handed by the detective himself. Gary would never talk to me about his case, but I once heard him telling Richard, "Hell, I'm just glad the guy didn't shoot my ass off. He could have gotten away with it easily enough, that's for sure."

Somehow some semblance of civilized life continued. Everyone shaved once a week in his own cell. A guard would come by and, for twenty-five cents, let you use the safety razor and brush. You used the brush to mix lather from soap and water in a half-pint milk carton. You shaved under the guard's supervision, then passed the tray back out to him when you were finished.

Milk cartons were handy things to have around. They were also used for ashtrays and for making hot chocolate. You made hot chocolate by crumbling a Milky Way, bought from the portable commissary, in hot water.

The inmates had a trick with toilet paper that I'd never seen before. They would twist up a roll of it, set it on the concrete floor, then set it afire. It made a beautiful flame that lasted a remarkably long time. The fire could be used to heat instant coffee, which was smuggled in by the trusties who delivered the meals.

Letter-writing was some help in passing time. I wrote Marilyn every day, Jenny and Kelly every day or so.

I knew the mail was being censored so I restricted most of my letters to generalities. There were so many things I wanted to tell Marilyn but couldn't. Much of what was on my mind, though, I wouldn't have written anyway, because it would only have added to her worries.

The letter-writing and letter-getting situation was terribly frustrating. I received a letter from Kelly, but the days passed and still no letter came from Jenny.

Before leaving home I'd half-heartedly teased Jenny that she'd be too busy with boys and books to write me. In a letter to Marilyn, I wrote, "Bless Kelly's heart for the letter I got today. Guess Jenny just hasn't had time to write."

Eventually I learned that Jenny had written me several letters, and every one of them was sent back. Marilyn told me later that Jenny, in tears, told her as one after another of her letters came back: "Daddy kept telling me I wouldn't write. Now he'll think I really didn't."

Though I wrote her daily, Marilyn received only two of my letters. She also wrote me daily, but I received only two letters from her. These are facts you learn later, when you're released and don't need outside hope any more.

I daydreamed a lot. Your body can be locked up, but if you're fortunate enough to fantasize, not your mind. I thought almost constantly of my family—of what they would be doing at that time of day, of whether they were safe. I wondered if the precautions I'd taken before leaving for prison had been adequate.

My last few weeks at home, after my final decision

against a further appeal, had been devoted to getting my home, family, and business in shape to get along without me. I sold Town and Country Pest Control to an Atlanta firm—for substantially less than it was worth. It had been an agonizing decision to sell the little business I had built up from scratch, but I had to find a way to provide for my family's financial needs while I was gone. I sold both the exterminating business and the contracting business under terms to provide a continuing income for them.

I then set about putting other matters in order. I prepared a detailed resume of my financial interests—every income and outgo. Marilyn referred to a schedule to learn what must be paid or would be received. I tried to anticipate unforeseen situations that might occur and planned for the proper parties to be notified to take care of them. I arranged to have all my insurance premiums paid automatically.

Concerned about the wide publicity my case had received, I made the house as secure as possible. Some deranged person, knowing I was away, might try to pull a prank, or worse. I bought strong new locks for all the doors, and wondered what happened to families of less able men than I.

That waiting period before I'd left for prison had been a time of doubt and indecision. I didn't know where I would be serving my sentence. Still pending against me was the twenty-three-count indictment; what disposition would be made of that? Would I be gone for a year and a day, or for several years?

I intentionally investigated prison life—I found out so many frightening things, that I didn't know what to expect. I'd received a lot of advice on what to do—how to conduct myself in prison, how to avoid danger. I had nightmares about what it would be like.

Marilyn and I tried not to think about it or talk about it. Of course, we thought and talked about little else. Every time Marilyn and I would touch hands, we'd suddenly find ourselves clutched in embrace, as if it were for the last time.

I spent most of the final days before leaving around the house. The girls were in school and so was Marilyn. She had begun teaching, the first full-time job she had held since we were married. We needed the money, and we had agreed that the job would help occupy her mind and time while I was away.

In the midday quiet of our four-bedroom suburban home, I did a lot of thinking and praying. I dreaded the ordeal ahead, not only for myself but also for all the suffering and embarrassment it would mean for Marilyn and the girls. Children can be viciously cruel at times without really meaning it. Would Jenny and Kelly, I wondered, be taunted because of their jailbird father?

I sat down with a tape-recorder and dictated a long, rambling, emotional message, leaving it to be played by Marilyn after I was gone. I tried to express many of the thoughts and feelings that were surging in me: my love for Marilyn—how much she had meant to me through all the good times and especially the bad; my concern for Jenny and Kelly, and my regret that they had, it seemed, gone through more rough times than any children should have to; my assurances (given with considerably more confidence than I felt) that everything would turn out all right, that I would be back home with them soon; and my final instructions on the details that would need attention while I was away. "It seems that so much of our time has been spent in explaining things to our daughters—Little Bill's death, Kathy," I said to Marilyn on the tape. "I know that the years right now are the most impressionable of their lives. . . . I hope they'll be able somehow to keep a cheerful outlook despite all that's happened. . . . I know that what you and the children are beginning to face is going to be a hard, long ordeal. Remember that you mean more to me than I can ever tell you . . ."

Two days before I left for prison, I drove 120 miles to Augusta to spend a soul-cleansing day with Kathy at the state center for mentally retarded children. I left there wondering how I could have been feeling so sorry for myself.

In my cell I recalled my last night in Macon, before my minister and I caught the plane for Texas. Friends and neighbors kept dropping in, most of them awkward but sincere in their remarks to me, unsure of what to say in such unusual circumstances but intent on making some expression of concern. It was a long, emotional evening, but one that gave me a deep and long-lasting awareness of how much people cared.

Red Smallwood came over that night. Red had

worked for me for twelve years. All his children are bright; I had helped one of them, Diane, get a scholarship to Macon Junior College while I was in the State Legislature. She stopped by the house that night with Red, and as they were about to leave she came over to me, and without a word, she put her arm around my neck and kissed my cheek. That said more to me than any words could have.

Charlie Norman said his goodbyes, and everything that had been welling up in my chest and throat all that day and night finally broke through. Charlie is a longtime business associate, and one of my dearest friends over the years. We stood there in the doorway, our arms around each other's shoulders, and just let the tears flow.

11

FOOTSTEPS BROUGHT ME BACK to the hard prison floor. Mike had a visitor. I'd been in jail almost a week, and it was the first time anyone had been to see him. He had made it a special point to ridicule others who had visitors and to boast about his self-sufficiency.

"I've got nobody, I don't need nobody, and I don't want nobody," he had announced one night. It was just after Danny's sister had been to see him. That visit seemed to anger Mike, as so many things did. He berated the young prisoner: "Your nursemaid's back again, is she? Can't make it all by yourself in the big, bad jail, eh sonny?" And so forth.

Nobody hazed Mike while he was being visited, of course. Most of the other men ignored him and his guest, an elderly, white-haired man rather shabbily dressed.

But something about the actions of the two caught my interest, and I sat against the door of the dayroom and watched them out of the corner of my eye.

The middle window of the three view-windows at the end of the dayroom was directly over the small steel door that opened for food to be passed through. The little steel door had apparently worn over a period of time, or else it didn't fit very well, because there was a slit about one-eighth of an inch deep at the top of the little door. If you bent down so that your eyes were level with the top of the opening—or sat, as I was doing—you could see the light coming through the tiny crack.

Visitor and prisoner stood facing each other through the middle window—made, of course, of unbreakable glass—and conversed by means of a speaker system.

As Mike and the other man spoke in low tones, I noticed a slight movement about the level of Mike's knees. His right hand was extended as far down as he could reach, and his fingers were even with the slit above the food door. Every few minutes his hand would reach back up to the front of his waist, then dip back down again.

I couldn't see anything of the visitor except his face, but I realized that he was slowly, casually feeding something through the little opening to Mike, who was tucking the contraband away inside the waistband of his trousers.

Later that day I noticed that Mike seemed to be acting peculiarly, almost as if he were drunk. "What's wrong with him?" I asked David.

"He's on dope."

Afterward I saw other inmates receiving something —drugs, most of the time—in the same manner Mike had. It was done very deftly. Unless you were looking for the exchange, you'd never know that anything strange was going on. Another exchange point, this one involving trusties, was a trash can in the hall at one end of the day-room. Prisoners could reach through the bars and drop things into it. They could also reach into it to get things out. Trusties emptied it daily.

I saw Gary put some money in the trash can one day, so I watched carefully when the trusty came. He put the money in his pocket and left a packet in the can. Gary got the packet a few minutes after the trusty left, opened it, and popped several pills into his mouth.

I'm reasonably sure that I was the only one in my tank who didn't use drugs of one kind or another during my stay in the tank. I saw almost all of the others taking them. Most swallowed them, with water, but Mike had a syringe—perhaps obtained through a trash-can exchange. Some drugs also were smuggled in through the food slot by trusties who brought the meals around. Prisoners who were not supplied by a visitor or a trusty bought drugs from another inmate using either money or favors.

Anyone in the tank who wanted to get high enough so that life would be more livable, could. And this was true even though the prison authorities were strict in try-ing to curtail the drug traffic. Apparently the authorities didn't want to be bothered with the bad publicity that could result from someone's taking an overdose of drugs.

There were frequent searches and shakedowns for the illicit pills and powders. The inmates, after receiving them one way or another, would flush the containers down the commode. If they didn't use all the drugs immediately, they hid them in the lining of their clothes, in a hollowed-out heel of their shoes, or even in their rectums, tied up in what looked like tiny polyethelene bags.

The guards were certainly onto these tricks. Perhaps they were bribed. They always missed looking in the little cranny under the top of the metal table, where Mike kept his syringe.

Mike tore the sleeves off his convict shirts and used them like a tourniquet around his upper arms to make the veins stand out before injecting the needle. He'd learned to knot the cloth with one or two deft movements, holding one end with his free hand, the other end with his teeth. Once or twice, when he was nervous and shaky—apparently coming off a high—he had to get Charlie or Richard to help him fasten the knot.

Shooting up seemed to relax Mike, to calm him down. He was like a different person when he was really high. I even got into one or two rational conversations with him at times like this. He talked slowly, seeming to drag words out—about how he would come to Georgia when he got out of jail and "do things for you." He seemed to envision me as some sort of crime kingpin, and himself as my number one henchman. "I'll take care of those guys who sent you up," he said a couple of times.

I would go along with him, of course, nodding agreement, trying to establish some kind of reasonable relationship with him.

Then the drugs would begin to wear off and he'd revert to type—the bullying, animalistic tank boss, harrassing me, pushing me as far as he could, never letting me relax, keeping me wondering if he was bluffing or if we were going to have a final reckoning.

In jail, where you're faced with idleness and monotony day after day, with no hope and no activity, everyone is on the lookout for anything that will help speed the hours by. Drugs, deviant sex, and violence all served this purpose to some extent.

The overwhelming obsession of all the men was sex. It was almost all they talked about. They constantly bragged about previous exploits—especially Mike and Charlie, who had sexual lying contests—and talked about all the new records they would set when they were released.

They didn't wait until they got out, though, to find relief of a sort.

It took several days before I began to get used to seeing them in the nude. Charlie, Richard, and Mike stayed completely naked most of the time. The others were usually bare from the waist up, their coveralls knotted around their waists.

If a man wanted to masturbate, I'd have thought he would prefer to do it at night in the privacy of his own cell. But they didn't wait for night. Mike, Charlie, and Richard—and sometimes Gary—often fondled their genitals without even seeming to think about it. They had no inhibitions about their sexual acts and no desire to hide them.

When I was a kid there was a game we played call "lagging to the line." You would draw a line in the dirt, then see who could toss a marble or a coin closest to it.

Mike, Charlie, and Richard had another version of "lagging to the line," played while masturbating. Only this time they used semen instead of marbles or coins.

And they had other forms of competition in which timing or swiftness was the deciding factor.

I felt that there must be a link between the educational background and sexuality of the prisoners. The better-educated men seemed to be more able to cope with their sexual drives. With the illiterates, some form of sexual relief seemed to be the overwhelming aim of their day-to-day, almost minute-to-minute, existence. In their peer group, it was a casual, accepted form of recreation and, I suppose, a tension reliever.

After the rape of Danny, I never felt safe from sexual assault. It took me a long while after entering the jail—until my bodily urges left me no choice—to make the decision to use the toilet. Even to urinate, you had to pull the coveralls off your shoulders and down around your knees. If the others felt like attacking you, this was a very vulnerable position to be in.

The whole time I was in the Tarrant County Jail, I went without bathing. For one thing, after I witnessed the rape of the kid, I didn't want to undress in front of the other men. For another, I wanted to keep myself as stinking and unattractive as possible. I didn't even wipe myself after bowel movements. I got so I could hardly stand to be around myself, and I was hoping nobody else could stand to be around me, either.

Next to sex, violence was the major outlet for the men in my tank. If one of them felt like beating up another one, he'd go right ahead and do it.

I had watched my share of fights as a youth and been in some myself, none of this had prepared me for the violence I encountered in jail.

Outside, if you're a spectator to a fight, you can move as close to the fighters or as far away as you choose. You can cheer for one to beat the other; you can congratulate the winner or commiserate with the loser.

In jail, you can never safely consider yourself a spectator. Your role is shaped by the bars and walls that restrict your movements and by the mood of the other fighters. If one of the combatants isn't faring very well, he might look for somebody else to tangle with. It could always be you. And even if you're the toughest guy in the cell, you can't be sure several of the others won't gang up on you.

There's a certain savagery in prison brawls that would horrify the most hardened male. The fighters seem to go almost insane with a lust for blood and an irrational desire to punish the opponent even after the fight has been decided. Not since grammar school days had I known the hatred a bully can arouse. I knew that feeling now as I saw Mike or Charlie, or both, brutalize one of the men, sometimes reducing them to tears as they begged for mercy.

In jail, you develop the habit of bracing yourself to keep from cowering and cringing every time one of the other inmates approaches. You never know when he will kick or spit at or hit you. Nerves become frayed from the strain. You learn to keep your back to a wall and your genitals, especially, well protected at all times.

The inmates seemed to keep their own inventories of the pain sustained, biding their time until an opportunity came for revenge. There were always two or more of the weaker ones—especially David and Gary—plotting in a corner of the dayroom to tell on their tormentors, trying to smuggle a note out in an attempt to get transferred to another tank. It never seemed to work.

The men in my cellblock would yell back and forth to those in adjoining ones. They had learned each other's names, although I don't suppose they'd ever seen one another.

"Hey, Joe," one of the inmates in my tank would holler, "you still over there?" And Joe would call back, "Naw, man, I'm visiting my girlfriend over in San Antone."

It seemed that there was almost always some kind of commotion in one of the nearby cellblocks. When a fight broke out we could hear the screaming and cursing quite plainly, and often there'd be a metallic "thunk!" as someone was thrown against the opposite side of our dayroom wall.

These disturbances worried me, because the violence often seemed to be contagious; a fight nearby would inspire someone in our tank to try to start one there.

I discovered that some inmates among the 148 on the seventh floor were worse off then I was, at least insofar as physical arrangements were concerned. Some of the cell-blocks held 24 or 30 men, and they would be locked up at night in groups of four rather than individually. I could imagine the homosexual activity—voluntary or forced—that this kind of arrangement must inspire. I heard some sounds during the night that reinforced my imaginings.

I also learned, from talk in my tank and from words and sounds that drifted into it, that racial fights between groups of whites and blacks were not uncommon in some of the tanks, especially the larger ones.

The other men in my tank, it seemed to me, had no hope, nothing on the outside to live for. Their one aim was to exist in the jail environment. If that meant stealing from another inmate, or beating him up, then that became their life style.

I often thought about state prisoners I had seen in Georgia working alongside the road. Even they seemed to be better off than we were. At least they were given some degree of freedom, some means of using their energy.

My fifth day in jail, Richard directed an obscenity at a passing guard. I don't know why he did it, unless he had had trouble with the guard previously. The guard left and returned minutes later with another one. They dragged

Richard out screaming, and he was gone for three days.

"They've taken him to the hole," David told me.

When the guards brought him back, they again had to drag him, but this time he wasn't protesting. He was too weak to walk.

I heard him telling another prisoner what it had been like. He said they'd dressed him in a short gown, like those used in hospitals for patients being prepped for surgery.

The hole, he said, was a small cell similar in shape and size to a casket standing on end. There were no lights, and once he was locked in, he was in total darkness. He was fed nothing but bread and water. There were no toilet facilities. He had to use the floor, then sit or stand in his own wastes.

He said that after the first day or so he'd gotten vertigo and couldn't tell whether he was upright or up-side-down.

After they brought him back to the dayroom, he lay on the floor, hardly moving, for more than half a day. When the evening meal came, he ate like a starving man and immediately heaved it all up. But he ate some more, kept it down, and the color began to return to his face. Finally he made it to the far end of the dayroom and, with David's help, managed to take a shower.

Before I had been in the Tarrant County Jail very long, I learned that anything in the world loses its shock value after awhile. At first all the modesty and decency that had been ingrained in me in my lifetime was outraged and horrified by the drug-taking, brutality, and sex-games I witnessed during my first few hours and days in the day-room. I was mortified and embarrassed for those taking part in the activities and fearful that they would expect me to join in.

But before long I realized that I had no alternative but to stay there and witness these things, and surprisingly, soon I became fairly well accustomed to what was happening. I never really became used to it, but I conditioned myself to a twilight zone existence in which the obscene was commonplace. It is amazing how the mind will react to previously unheard-of circumstances and train itself to accept whatever it must.

To notice the complete unconcern of the guards about what happened in the tanks was most unnerving. The guards were protected from the violent prisoners, but I—an inmate myself—was not. The guards never made any attempt to discipline the prisoners. In fact, I suspected that they might pass the time of day by watching the fights and sexual activities from some secluded location.

I felt so many times that if the jailer would just come by once in awhile and look in or say something, this would help ease the tension. But nobody came by; nobody checked. Nobody cared.

If a guard did happen past—and this was rare indeed—his remarks seemed intended to humiliate or enrage the inmates, not encourage them. The guards could call an inmate any obscene name they wanted to, but let a prisoner try the same thing on a guard and he was in serious trouble.

I was disturbed by the unfairness of what was happening. I and the other inmates had been sent to jail as punishment for crimes. And being sent to jail should be punishment enough, it seemed. But to be punished while there—mentally or physically or both—was beyond all fairness.

To be so mistreated, and so inhumanly treated, adds to the measure of punishment beyond anything that is justified and is what ultimately breaks a prisoner down. It's a major emotional upheaval to be put in jail, and then to be treated no better than a mad dog while you're there destroys any incentive to repent.

Perhaps when you're first jailed you might feel contrite. But then you are urinated on and fed inedible slop, the guards and other prisoners insult you with obscenities, and the other prisoners assault you verbally, if not physically, while the guards and prison officials do absolutely nothing to protect you. This creates a sense of injustice and a desire for revenge—just the opposite of what's intended.

If you lock a fine hunting dog in a cage and jab him with pointed sticks, when he's released he's going to bite the first person he can. I am sure that the main motivation for many prisoners is the desire for vengeance, usually directed toward the jailer, guard, or other prison officials, and sometimes toward another prisoner. When the prisoner is released, this desire for revenge is unleashed on the unsuspecting public—perhaps fed with the prisoner's conscious knowledge that the public allows what is happening in jail or perhaps with only a vague determination to take revenge on the first available victim. The average prisoner feels that the public is apathetic about what happens to him after he is imprisoned. I can understand this feeling after being there.

I am not prepared to state with any assurance whatsoever that I would not have resorted to drugs if I'd been forced to live in the tense atmosphere of the Tarrant County Jail much longer.

12

LOOKING BACK, as I did so frequently, I realized that I had run for election to the Georgia Legislature with no hint of support from the Macon political power structure. This group of powerful individuals had studiously ignored me during my campaign. But then, after I'd won, they suddenly became "infatuated" with me. Marilyn and I found ourselves invited to the country club, I was a welcome figure at the Courthouse and City Hall, and my back was slapped by well-heeled citizens as I walked the downtown streets.

In many cases, the next time I saw the backslappers was in my hotel room in the state capitol, where they came to implore me to support certain special interest legislation that would be of benefit to them.

Early in my first term, I was able to accomplish one of my major goals in the House. Under long-established policy, appropriations bills—bills providing how much money the state will spend and how it will be divided—are usually hammered into final form in the Appropriations Committee. But I was not a member of the committee, and had little influence with any of its members. Rarely is an appropriations bill altered once it reaches the floor of the House. But with a lot of hard work, I won a successful vote on an amendment to provide both additional operating funds and capital outlay funds for Gracewood State School and Hospital. This would provide room for more children and improve the quality of their care.

By this time, Kathy had been admitted to the hospital, but many children like her still remained on the waiting list.

During the second year of my two-year term, the country club invitations gradually began falling off. Not surprisingly, my fall from favor with the local power structure more or less coincided with my developing reputation as a hard-nosed maverick who refused to bow to pressure—or, as I preferred to be called, an independent legislator. I refused to kowtow to the power structure members and their requests—which often sounded more like demands—on how I should vote on specific bills. It seemed incredible that this was a part of my life too as I thought back in my prison cell.

At about that time, I was stepping on some very influential toes in Macon by investigating dummy corporations established to buy land on the routes of interstate highways or into future urban renewal projects, which were then quietly dissolved after the land was sold for handsome profits.

In 1964, I was reelected without opposition, but in 1965, after reapportionment of the House, I had to run again in a special election. This turned out to be the year of the Republicans in Bibb County, following Barry Goldwater's sweeping victories in Georgia and Bibb County a year earlier. And I was a Democrat, all the way.

That year the GOP qualified candidates for all eight legislative posts in Bibb County—six House seats and two in the Senate. When the returns were in, Republicans had chalked up victories in every race but one—mine. I had just squeaked by with a two-vote margin over a likable young candidate named John Stewart.

Or had I?

Stewart demanded a recount. This time, after the tally, I trailed him—by three votes. It was obvious that I was about to become embroiled in another of the controversies which the local press would later say "helped to make the name 'Laite' a household word in Bibb County." I'd never been one to back out of a fight. I let it be known that I planned to take the election dispute to court.

That was when I learned the full extent of my fall from grace with the men and organizations that run things in Bibb County and Macon. No law firm would accept my case.

I went to see a young lawyer who had helped me get

elected. He averted his eyes, explaining that he was just "too busy" to take the case. I went to see a lawyer who had once served in the House and whom I considered a political as well as personal friend. Before I could explain the reason for my visit, he pulled out a three-by-five index card from his desk drawer and showed it to me. It was a short inter-office memo: "Don't get involved in the Laite-Stewart case." It had been signed by a senior member of his law firm.

Finally, I went to see Hank O'Neal. Like me, O'Neal had a reputation as a maverick. He often took on unpopular cases, many of which appeared to be hopeless, and he won more than his share of them.

When I called O'Neal, he said in his blunt, straight-to-the-point way, "You must have already called every other law firm in town."

"You're pretty close," I admitted. "None of them will take my case, and I've got to have a lawyer at the courthouse by five o'clock today if I'm going to contest the election. Will you do it?"

"I'll see you there at a quarter to five," he said, and hung up the phone.

I entered the courthouse that afternoon before O'Neal arrived, and was met by two prominent Bibb County Republicans. "Well, Laite," one said, "I guess you couldn't get yourself a lawyer, huh?"

O'Neal had walked up just in time to hear the remark.

"I'm his damn lawyer," he growled. "What's it to you?"

That ended the conversation.

The case was a strange one. It went to the Georgia Court of Appeals, which ruled 7-2 in my favor. But before I could begin rejoicing, Stewart's attorney asked for a rehearing, and it was granted.

A few days after granting Stewart a rehearing, the Georgia Court of Appeals reversed itself and unanimously ruled for him. That gave the Republican the election victory.

In 1966, I bounced back strong and was reelected to the General Assembly, garnering 15,530 votes to 14,453 for a Republican named Hunter Johnson, although Republicans held on to a majority of the Bibb legislative seats.

My thoughts rambled back to the events that put me in prison. My exterminating business had been formed in 1959 and it was doing exceedingly well. The Small Business Set-Aside Program established by the Kennedy administration giving preference to small businesses in the procurement of government contracts helped. Because of the program, I was able to successfully bid and perform a number of exterminating contracts for different federal agencies throughout the country.

Later, the method of awarding these contracts was changed so that I was put in the position of a subcontractor, doing the exterminating work for a general contractor who handled the construction part of the job. This change cut into my profits and also into my performance, since I was being regulated by a general contractor.

Convinced that I could supervise carpenters, painters, and plumbers as well as I could supervise exterminators, I formed a subsidiary—Laite Contracting Company. This enabled me to bid a whole job, bidding the construction as the prime contract, then subcontracting the electrical, plumbing, and other jobs. I still handled the exterminating work through my own company.

I knew I would have some difficulties going into a field that was foreign to me. But I understood government regulations, or thought I did. I had attended seminars and short-courses to help me and my employees understand and follow government requirements for construction jobs.

So I began bidding construction jobs, and one of them was the Big Springs, Texas, project, which involved sixty run-down houses in an FHA subdivision. The contract called for rehabilitating the houses—in some cases, practically rebuilding them—so they would again be livable.

We were finished with the job when I returned to the General Assembly in January, 1967, for my first session after being elected in 1966. My problems had already begun.

It became obvious that I was going to have trouble collecting all the money owed me under the contract.

I filed the required invoice with the FHA's field office in Lubbock, Texas. Months went by with no response. After several unsuccessful attempts to break the money loose from the government, I went to Washington with my attorney, and we called on the contracting officer for the FHA. After listening to our arguments, he approved a $10,000 payment on the balance.

Attempts to obtain the remaining $30,000 plus other claims against government agencies met with silent refusal. Finally, the reason given for the holdout was that landscaping provisions of the contract had not been performed.

The agreement had required topsoil to be placed and graded, grass was to be planted on each plot of land. I had subcontracted with a nursery in Big Springs, and in my opinion a completely satisfactory job had been done. I took color photos of each piece of property, showing the completed landscaping. The green grass in the photos was indisputable. I took the prints to the FHA. Still they refused to pay, giving evasive answers when I asked why.

I began to strengthen my requests. I called on my congressman, Rep. John J. Flynt, Jr., and in a strongly-worded letter he demanded that the FHA pay me.

Still no payment was made.

My attorney and I made another trip to Washington. This time the FHA contracting officer showed that he was becoming a little annoyed with us. "Mr. Laite," he said, "when it's inevitable that you're going to be raped, you might as well relax, son, and enjoy it." He refused to elaborate on why the money was being withheld.

A few days later, Rep. Flynt notified my attorney that

he had received a letter from the FHA indicating that a grand jury investigation of my company's performance on the Big Springs Project was impending.

After all the delays and refusals to pay, this was the only word I received of the investigation, and even this was second hand.

My lawyer and I went directly to Dallas and met with two government attorneys, who finally acknowledged that an investigation was forthcoming. They said it would center on what they described as "170 labor law violations." A representative of the U.S. Department of Labor was there, but he refused to give us any details on what the alleged violations involved, other than to say that they were criminal violations and that the government planned to seek an indictment.

While I was involved in the General Assembly session, I heard unofficially that a grand jury in Lubbock had begun an investigation of the case. After much deliberation I decided to go to Lubbock and appear before the grand jury—something I wasn't required to do—and lay all my cards on the table. I felt I had nothing to hide.

On March 8 I went before the jury and stayed before them most of the day. Twenty-three men and women on the jury and two government attorneys interviewed me at length. I had all my records and files pertinent to the Big Springs job spread out on a long conference table there in the courtroom. I told the questioners that if there was anything they wanted to know, I would be glad to tell them; if there were any figures they needed, I would gladly supply them.

The following week I learned that the grand jury had declined to indict me.

13

NOT UNTIL I WAS QUESTIONED before the Lubbock grand jury did I learn specifically what the government charges were.

The questioning by the government attorneys dealt primarily with overtime, which three employees on the Big Springs job contended they should have been paid but weren't. The employees, I learned, were from Macon, men who had worked for me on several previous jobs.

There also seemed to be some doubt about whether all terms of the contract had been fulfilled. Had the proper amount of felt been placed under the roofing? Was the correct plumbing installed? Had the government been short-changed on the material?

These were questions the answers to which even I was not absolutely certain. Big Springs, Texas, is a long way from Macon, Georgia. I'd tried to spend as much time on the project as I could, but there was my legislator's business to attend to. Most of the work on the Big Springs job had been done in the summer of 1965. That was the same period during which I'd been involved in the lost election battle. So I had really spent very little time on the site of the Texas project. Truthfully, I was on the site less than six times during the six months the job was in progress.

In the construction field, temporary help is used almost every day, on an hour-to-hour or a day-to-day basis. You try to hire competent foremen to supervise the job in your absence, but the reliability of such hired help is always in doubt.

I had to rely on the word of my foreman and superintendent that the job had been performed to specifications. They had convinced me that it had; and together we had apparently convinced the Lubbock grand jury.

That jury investigated the case for two weeks; they subpoenaed every supervisor, every subcontractor, every supplier, every laborer—in short, everyone in any way affiliated with the job. They had the benefit of my records and my full day's testimony before them—testimony given, incidentally, over my attorney's objections. He had advised me against appearing before the grand jury, but it was my view that the government's only desire was to make a full and fair appraisal of the project and get to the bottom of the allegations against me, and that I could be of help to them in doing so.

So the grand jury studied my case thoroughly. I was, in effect, tried—albeit one-sidedly. There is nothing impartial about a grand jury hearing. All the evidence is presented by the prosecution. There is no defense attorney and little or no defense. The assignment of the grand jury is solely and specifically to determine if enough evidence exists to take the case to court.

If the government feels constrained to take a case to a grand jury, it can usually get an indictment. Not so in my case—the jury, after considering all the evidence, refused to indict me.

But the U.S. Constitution's double jeopardy clause does not apply to grand jury proceedings as it does to regular jury trials where a "not guilty" verdict is final. My exhilaration over the Lubbock grand jury's decision was short-lived. Six months later, I learned that another grand jury was preparing to investigate the Big Springs Project.

The government, it seemed, was determined to get an indictment.

My disappointment was mixed with bewilderment at the government's attitude. Not that I could swear that the Big Springs contract had been fulfilled 100 percent. Government specifications are highly technical, often ambiguous, sometimes conflicting. Many times it is difficult to determine exactly what should be done on a given job.

This does not have to be an insurmountable problem. There are the seminars and precontract conferences aimed at explaining all aspects of a job. And if, after all this, there is still some shortcoming, the two sides can easily move administratively to correct problems.

This had happened to my company. In other contracts I had fulfilled for the government—Army, Navy, or civilian agencies—there were minor problems in the area of wages and overtime, for example. Always before, the government would ask me to check my records. If an error was found, I would make restitution; if not, I would submit proof of satisfactory payment and that would be the end of it.

But in this case, the FHA refused to allow me such administrative relief. In fact, they would not even tell me where I had supposedly failed to comply. Rather than remedy any mistake I might have made, the FHA seemed intent on sending me to jail.

In Dallas, about four hundred miles from Lubbock, the second grand jury was drawn.

I went to Dallas with my attorney, prepared to testify before this grand jury, too. As I was about to enter the hearing room, a government attorney informed my lawyer that this time an indictment would be sought not only for the other alleged violations but also for perjury allegedly committed before the Lubbock grand jury.

As the man walked away, my lawyer grabbed my arm. "Listen, Bill," he said, "don't go in there. If you've got to deal with rascals like this, then deal with them in a courtroom."

This time I listened to his advice. I had seen in Lubbock how a lawyer can twist the facts to suit his own purposes; how he can, if he's clever, throw a witness off balance, make him answer without thinking through the question.

The second grand jury spent less time investigating the case than the first had. And this time, the decision was different. They returned two long indictments: one charging me with twenty-three counts of labor violations, defrauding the government, and failure to fulfill terms of the contract; the other charging me with five counts of perjury in connection with my testimony before the Lubbock grand jury.

It took me a while to fully comprehend the impact of it. I had been confident this grand jury would reach the same conclusions as the other had. I began, slowly, to absorb the consequences of the indictments. I could not make myself think about the trial I must face. The charges in the indictments would, I knew, be spread over the front pages of the local papers the next day. My first concern was how this would affect my family, but I also feared the affect on my company, the business reputation I had built up over eight long years.

My company had been doing business with the government for several years. All the previous contracts had been accepted as having been fulfilled satisfactorily. Before a company can do work for the government on a bid basis, it must produce proof of competency, and this I had done on more than one occasion.

Any man doing business in the contracting field has

to put up three "C's"—Character, Capability, and Capital—and he has to have performance and payment bonds executed before the work can even begin. Then in the event the contractor defaults, there is an insurance company that underwrites payment to all parties who suffer.

Before a contractor can obtain these bonds, he must prove himself both capable and honest—that he is respected in his business field and community. Before he can get funds to finance a project, he must prove both his integrity and his capability to perform the work.

But let one allegation be made—just one—and all that is shot to pieces. Let twenty-eight allegations be made, and it is obliterated. A reputation for honesty, integrity, for capable work performance can be destroyed almost as completely by an accusation made as by one proved.

On the day the grand jury returned the indictments, I knew that my effectiveness as a contractor was doomed.

The government used the tactic of delay. My case was delayed month after month, in an apparent effort to deplete my funds. If they thought I would give in and plead guilty, they were mistaken.

Not that I hadn't considered it. The mental anguish over my son's recent death, the long delays and mounting costs, the adverse publicity affected me badly, and I was seriously considering giving up.

After one of many sleepless nights, I placed a long distance call to my attorney in Dallas, William Fonville. "Bill," I said, "the hell with it. I'm ready to quit. I've had

145

this thing hanging over me and my family long enough. I just want to get it over with. I'm ready to plead guilty, take whatever they give me."

"Bill, you'd better think a long time before you do that," Fonville told me. "You plead guilty or *nolo contendre*—either one—and more than likely you'll end up with five or ten years in prison."

"Five or ten years!" I couldn't believe what I was hearing. "But—that's crazy! It's ridiculous!"

"Judge Leo Brewster doesn't think so," Fonville said. Then he told me about the judge in my case. Leo Brewster, he informed me, had a far-reaching reputation for fairness—but also for toughness. He apparently believed in punishment as a deterrent, and consistently handed out stiff sentences.

So we went to trial.

We went to trial, not on charges of violations in connection with the work done in Big Springs, but on charges of perjury.

I have, in fact, never been tried on any of the counts alleging twenty-three violations in carrying out the Big Springs work. The government instead arranged to have me tried on the indictment charging five counts of perjury stemming from my testimony before the Lubbock grand jury.

14

MY TRIAL BEGAN on May 11, 1968, in Lubbock, Texas, where the U.S. district courtroom is in the old federal post office building.

I didn't believe the government could win its case, but my attorneys, Fonville and Bill Evans of Lubbock, told me that the prosecution had built itself a good case around the Lubbock grand jury proceedings.

The indictment charged that I had lied when I told the Lubbock grand jury that:

1. My company had bought, ordered, and paid for sufficient felt and roofing material to cover the roofs of the sixty houses in the project with the required two layers of felt. (The government claimed that I had not and that, in fact, the houses had been covered with only one layer.)

2. An initial plumbing contract had covered all plumbing requirements of the contract. (The government alleged that all the required plumbing had not been installed, and that the plumbing subcontractor and one of his employees had informed me of this.)

3. I did not advise that certain laborers or mechanics could work in excess of forty hours in certain weeks and would be paid straight wages rather than an overtime rate. (The government claimed three men had worked overtime and had been paid regular rates.)

4. A room had been taken from a house in the project and locked into another house turned around, and then I'd had to take legal recourse to get it back. (According to the government's investigation, this had not been done.)

My attorneys and I agreed that the government's strongest case concerned the overtime pay; count three.

It was during the government's investigation of the overtime allegations that my wife and I first came into contact with the FHA's investigators and learned that these gentlemen sometimes perform their duties in rather strange and unorthodox ways.

My wife was secretary-treasurer of Town and Country Pest Control. She had been alone in the office one afternoon when two men came in and identified themselves as representatives of the Federal Housing Administration.

"We're just here to see what we can do to help you, Mrs. Laite," one of them had told her, smiling. "We understand the problems y'all have been having collecting money that's owed you for some of the work you've done for us. Now, if you'll just let us look over your records, we think we can go ahead and get this whole business straightened out."

"Well, we'll certainly appreciate anything you can do," Marilyn told them, and led them to our filing cabinets.

What they were really looking for, it turned out, was evidence they could use to put me behind bars. On the basis of their false story, my wife unlocked all our files and records and allowed them to make themselves at home.

They remained there for three days, their noses buried deep in our business.

And they soon stopped acting like invited guests. When Marilyn could not immediately put her hands on a particular document they wanted to examine, they became impatient and disrespectful. They began coupling intimidation with deceit.

"It would be awfully dumb of you to try to hide anything from us," Marilyn recalls one of them snapping after she had taken several minutes to locate a misplaced file.

The third day they were there, I returned to the office and was accorded the same unpleasant treatment.

Since then I have learned that any time a government agency wants to see the records of a private company, the agency's representatives are required by law to identify themselves and state the nature of their business, even to the point of acknowledging that their object is a criminal indictment, if indeed it is. If there's something the company doesn't want them to see, it has the right to deny access to it. The proper course then is for the agency to go the route of the subpoena.

After this episode, I was hardly surprised during the trial when a witness testified that a government investigator, whom he identified, had threatened him.

The government was determined to get a conviction, no matter what means it had to employ or how much money it had to spend. I believe the reason for this was summed up exceedingly well by Judge Brewster, in his charge to the jury. Here are some excerpts from that charge:

"We have a project here that the FHA had financed and had to take over, and some of it was almost in a state of ruin from vandalism and neglect and other reasons. We all know what the testimony was in this case.

"The FHA had a white elephant on its hands.

"Mr. Laite made a contract to do some of those houses over and put them back in livable condition. Apparently he did not have the organization to handle that kind of work. His company which took on the job had been in the pest control business. He hired men he had never known before—a sheet metal worker to take charge of the property. As far as the evidence shows here, he had never done anything but sheet metal work, and had never been in charge of construction before. Mr. Laite brought him out here and put him in charge of the job. . . .

"Sargent, the foreman, took over control of the job. He was lax about his plumbing contractor, and he was lax about the roofing. There is no question about the fact that the job was loosely handled. It is not up to us to say whether Mr. Laite suffered along with some of the others or not. The job was not run like it would have been if he had been on it. But he is not being tried for that."

(I might interject here that if the government wants to charge me with hiring the wrong people to run the Big Springs job, I will here and now plead guilty.)

Continuing the judge's charge: "Another reason I say this case is loaded with dynamite is because unquestionably the FHA has been neglectful in its duties. It is hard to see how plumbing work like this got by when they had an inspector, or a man hired to inspect it out there. It is hard to see how roofing work that was put on those houses got by when the FHA had an inspector hired to go out there. I can not imagine anything more lax than an inspector telling the folks on the job that he would be out there on every Monday morning. They ought not to have known when the inspector was coming, and he ought not to have come at regular intervals. He ought to have come at times when they were not expecting him. Certainly, when he got there, he ought to have been able to find some of the things that happened in this case.

"Under those circumstances, in a government agency there is a strong tendency to look for 'goats'."

(Members of the jury, weren't you listening *at all* when the judge said that?!?)

151

The judge went on: "Somebody has to pay so as to take the spotlight off them. That may account for this evidence here of Montez that he was threatened as a witness. I do not approve of that and I know you do not either. That is not the conduct we have a right to expect from government agents. He testified to that, and he pointed the FHA man out right here in the courtroom that he said threatened him. That man sat in the courtroom and he is still sitting here, and he has not taken the witness stand yet to deny it or to explain it.

"You have not heard from the inspector. I do not know why. I do not know how he could explain one ply of felt out there, if he thought the contract called for two plies."

I should point out that Judge Brewster went on to note that the jury was not trying whether or not a good job had been done on the Big Springs project; and, if not, whose fault it was—mine or the FHA's, or both. What was at issue was my testimony before the Lubbock grand jury.

Nevertheless, I was confident—almost exuberant— by the time Judge Brewster finished his charge. To me, a layman, his charge sounded like the next thing to a directed acquittal.

My trial lasted five days. The jury acquitted me on count two, the one dealing with the plumbing subcontract. After the jury was unable to reach a verdict on count one, dealing with the felt applied to the roofs, the judge dismissed this count.

The jury returned a verdict of guilty on counts three and four.

My attorneys and I felt strongly that the judge should have thrown out count four on the basis of immateriality. Fonville had argued this point strongly to Judge Brewster. In fact, during the presentencing hearing, Fonville told the judge: "If your honor please, I submit it just couldn't even be relevant to the inquiry, much less material."

However, the judge overruled the motion to dismiss the count.

Some background is necessary concerning my comment to the grand jury on count four, the "turned around room." As Fonville pointed out to Judge Brewster, my remarks actually constituted an unresponsive answer to a question asked by a grand juror. By "unresponsive" my attorney meant that my answer—as a matter of fact, the question as well—was not even on the subject the grand jury was talking about.

The discussion had wandered momentarily to vandalism which, as evidence fully showed, had plagued the Big Springs project. The dialogue involving me and a grand juror went like this, the transcript shows:

Juror: "Mr. Laite, I would like to come back to this for just a minute. On this job in Big Springs, why—you inferred that after these houses were worked on, that they were pilfered or that there was damage to the houses as you would go from one house to another. Did I get you right on that?"

Laite: "Yes, sir."

Juror: "You would have evidence of that?"

Laite: "Yes, sir."

Juror: "All right, if you—"

Laite: ". . . In fact we had two instances out there where one house was vacant so long that the neighbors actually took one room off the house and turned it around and locked it into theirs, and we had to obtain legal recourse to get the thing back. . . ."

The trial jury found that that statement constituted perjury.

As Judge Brewster had cautioned the jury, an important element of perjury is that "the false testimony, if it was false, was knowingly and willfully given by the accused." The judge added that testimony could be given which was later proven false, "but when it comes to a charge of perjury, that is not enough. If the person believed that the statement was true, or if it happened to be made recklessly, or if the untrue statement was made due to neglect or to bad information, even though it was false, the person making it cannot be convicted of perjury unless he knew it was false."

I submit that my remark concerning a turned-around room was, first, immaterial; and, second, was made recklessly.

The grand jury proceeding in Lubbock had been an extremely tiring, mentally draining ordeal. After it was over, I slept for almost a day and a half. I had been on the stand for almost an entire day; many of the grand jurors had questioned me extensively. The facts they were inte-

154

rested in were more than two years old, and I'd had to rack my brains trying to remember what had occurred. The government attorneys had grilled me and grilled me and grilled me. They insinuated, they accused, they tried to confuse. They exhausted me completely, trying to make me answer rashly. And by the time the question of the turned-around room had come up, that's exactly what I did.

I had made a rash statement which, considered literally, was untrue. What I was trying to get across was that in this FHA project of three hundred houses, of which we were renovating sixty, people were living in houses that did not belong to them. There was an instance, which I'd had in the back of my mind when I made the statement about the turned-around room, where two families had built a covered rampway between two houses, and the alteration had been so extensive that it was difficult to tell later which rooms went with which house. We had to get legal authorization to tear the ramp down.

The guilty verdict on count three had been much less surprising. This count dealt with the allegation that I had told certain laborers they could work more than forty hours a week and still get straight wages rather than overtime pay.

Three employees from Macon who had gone to Big Springs to work for me on the FHA project later claimed to have worked eighteen to twenty hours a day, seven days a week, for twenty-three weeks, and that I had told them they could do so but that they would not be paid overtime wages.

It is a fact that I had agreed for the three men to work more than forty hours a week, for straight wages, and I have no doubt that they did work more than forty hours some weeks, although I doubt seriously that they ever worked the back-breaking schedules they claimed. Nevertheless, to my knowledge, they did not qualify for overtime pay under the agreement I had made with them.

They had been in Big Springs with nothing to do on the weekends, and wanted to use the time to make some extra money. They had called me, and I'd agreed to let them do some extra work on a piecemeal, subcontract basis. Such an arrangement, under the law, does not require the payment of overtime wages.

On Saturdays and Sundays, the men were to take old window screens off the project houses, transport them off the project site by truck, and repair and repaint them at the rate of $1 per screen.

What I did not find out until much later was that when they had returned to the project site with the first batch of screens, they ran into considerable trouble trying to fit the screens back in the windows. Some would fit only the windows they originally came from, and trying to match them up became an all but impossible puzzle.

So, they began repairing and repainting the screens there on the job site where they could be easily and quickly reinstalled.

However, as my lawyers and I interpreted the Davis-

Bacon Act, for me to have been guilty of violating it, I would have had to agree for the men to work overtime hours with no overtime pay, and I had entered into no such agreement with them. I felt that in a strict sense I had not violated the law because I had not known that the men had done the work on the job site.

However, even at the time I told the men they could do the piece work, I knew, without really giving it much thought, that they might not do it in a strictly legal manner.

This did not concern me. In previous jobs I had done for the government, there had been no insistence that the letter of the law be carried out. If a regulation was stretched or bent a little bit, the opportunity was always given to smooth things out administratively. I assumed that the same would be true in regard to the Big Springs project.

One purpose of the Davis-Bacon Act's overtime provisions is to discourage a contractor from working a man more than eight hours a day or 40 hours a week; to encourage him to spread the federal funds around, to hire more people, and in that way, to reduce unemployment. I knew I was violating this part of the law's intent; that is, I was violating the spirit of the law.

Even so, the government's action against me came as a total surprise. The three men had made no request for overtime pay while the work was in progress. There was a superintendent on the job. There were time badges. Workers were clocked in and out. Every contractor doing business with the government is required to execute weekly payroll compliances, and this we did. These forms certify the number of employees, names and addresses, classification and rate of pay, and number of hours worked. Each employer must sign the forms. Signing a false report subjects an employer to fine or imprisonment or both.

The three complainants signed every form, stating without exception that they had worked no more than eight hours a day, no more than forty hours a week—only to testify later that what they had signed was false.

The three men who testified that I had told them they could work overtime but at straight wages, and who claimed they had in fact worked many hours of overtime but received only regular pay were John Glover, Walter Lee Jackson, and Jim Lee Jackson. Glover was the key witness. His was the most damaging testimony against me.

Shortly after I'd learned the government was seeking an indictment against me, I had retained an organization comprising ex-FBI agents who were trained in investigation and in taking testimony and depositions from witnesses. Having worked part-time with the FBI while in college, I had great faith in the ability of the organization's agents and former agents.

The main investigator with the firm, and the one who did the work on my case, was Bill Murphy. A deliberate-speaking, slow-moving man, Murphy possessed a razor-sharp mind trained by his investigative work for the FBI. Murphy, now sixtyish, had served for nineteen of his twenty-five years with the bureau as special agent in charge of various field offices.

I didn't know what my position was relative to the government investigation. I had been at the job site so little and had relied so heavily on what my supervisor told me that I had no way of being certain whether or not any laws had, in fact, been broken. So I paid Murphy $100 a day plus expenses to find out for me. I told him I wanted the facts—good, bad, or indifferent. If I or my company had been wrong, I wanted to know it, and wanted to know it as soon as possible.

I supplied Murphy with a list of all my employees on the Big Springs job, and he conducted a detailed investigation that required months to complete. He visited the job site. He interviewed laborers, supervisors, subcontractors—anyone even incidentally affiliated with the project.

After completing the Texas phase of his probe, I told him about the three men who had worked in Big Springs and on other jobs for me.

He flew immediately to Macon and interviewed the three men. Here is what Murphy's report said about his talk with them:

"John Elijah Glover, Walter Lee Jackson, and Jimmy Lee Jackson, the latter's brother, were interviewed at Jimmy Jackson's residence on December 8, 1966, from approximately 7:30 to 9:00 p.m. . . . Glover, who acts as spokesman for the three, advised that an FHA man from Texas who came to see the three of them in the summer of 1966 said that some of the fellows who had worked on the Big Springs job complained they were not paid for the work they did, and asked if they had been paid properly. Glover claims that he told him to talk to Mr. Laite about the matter. He does not recall that any of them signed any statement or any paper at any time in connection with their conversation with this individual. Both Jimmy and Walter Jackson concurred. Glover claims that he followed Walter and Jimmy out to Big Springs to work, and that he went out there with the understanding that if there were any extra work to be done, it was to be done off the premises on weekends when they normally didn't have anything else to do, and that he would be compensated at the regular rate of pay because Mr. Laite had told him the job 'didn't have enough money in it to pay time and a half.'

"Glover said this was the understanding under which he went out there to work, and he has no complaint about the fact that he was paid at this rate for the hours which he put in. Glover related that he came back to Macon two or three times to see Laite and asked him for the money for the extra work, and he was given checks based on the amount of time which Sargent (job superintendent William Sargent) had put on the timecard for him for the extra work."

So Glover had told Murphy. At the trial, however, Glover denied making such statements to Murphy and alleged that I had entered into an agreement with him and the Jackson brothers for them to work overtime on the job site and yet be paid straight wages for the overtime work.

It was partially on the strength of Murphy's findings that I had decided to appear before the Lubbock grand jury. Only later did we learn the allegations about overtime given the FHA by these three men had been what had started all the trouble in the first place.

The law provides that a person cannot be convicted of perjury unless the falsity of his statement is proven by two credible witnesses or by one credible witness strongly corroborated by independent material.

A credible witness is one worthy of belief.

Was John Glover a credible witness?

Glover is well known by law enforcement officers in Macon and Bibb County—and not just because he once served a short time as a Bluecoat Officer in the Macon Police Department.

He had been arrested during the late 1950's for civil rights activities. Later, he was hired by the Police Department. While a Bluecoat Officer, he was caught red-handed trying to steal tires and lawnmowers from a Macon store, entered a plea of guilty, and went to prison. He was on parole from this felony offense when he testified against me.

Several months after testifying against me, Glover was arrested again, this time for stealing lumber from a Macon lumber company; and he served time for that offense.

I have recently learned that the "long arm" of the

FHA dabbled in the lumber case. Two officials of the lumber company called me, independently. Both said the same thing—representatives of the FHA had visited them and tried to prevail upon them to drop the case against Glover.

The FHA, without doubt, was trying to keep Glover's shabby record from deteriorating any further, in case he was needed to testify against me again. And it is a fact that the FHA later tried, without success, to build another case against me in connection with jobs my company had performed in Georgia.

I have also learned in recent months from two reputable Bibb County men who had worked for me in previous political campaigns that they, too, had visits from FHA agents before my trial. The FHA had tried to obtain statements from these two men claiming that I had asked them to persuade Glover to change his testimony against me.

15

IT HAD BEEN a highly technical case. The jurors had not seemed to exert themselves to understand it. They were inattentive; they lost interest. One old gentleman on the jury brazenly took noisy naps while the case was in progress, and other jurors found it more entertaining to joke about him among themselves than to pay attention to the testimony.

Damaging evidence in the case were the timecards which William Sargent, Jr., superintendent for the Big Springs job, kept for the three men and later turned over to the FHA. Sargent claimed the timecards indicated legitimate overtime I owed, but for which I had paid the painters regular wages. I had never seen the cards.

The jury of eight men and four women began deliberating my case at 2:53 p.m., Thursday, May 16, 1968. I waited with my wife and attorneys in a witness room across the hall from the courtroom. None of us felt confident enough to predict which way the verdict would go.

After recessing for the night, the jury resumed deliberations Friday morning at 9:00 o'clock. At 2:17 p.m., after approximately seven hours of deliberation over a two-day period, the jury made its decision. I cannot say that I was really surprised when the jury convicted me on two counts.

The judge asked me to stand and I did, somewhat shakily, to hear him say he would release me on my personal recognizance and sentence me later.

I began to visualize on the short but dreary plane ride back to Macon the repercussions my conviction would have in my hometown.

Even while I was on trial, a Macon newspaperman had called me in Fort Worth to ask my reaction to a development that clearly was related to my difficulties with the government. Marshall Keen—a former employee, a fraternity brother, a man I considered a close personal friend—had announced he would run for a seat in the Georgia House of Representatives. The seat he proposed to capture was mine.

If a friend would do something like that, I thought, what could I expect from my enemies?

About a month later, I returned to Dallas and again stood before Judge Brewster. In severe terms, after lecturing me on the seriousness of perjury, he sentenced me to a year and a day in the penitentiary.

The sentence seemed severe, particularly since it was the type from which no parole was possible. The entire year and a day would have to be served in prison. However, having heard of some much more severe sentences imposed by Judge Brewster, I was somewhat relieved.

My attorney served notice of appeal. He felt sure that we had excellent grounds. The appeal was filed.

Time crept by while the Fifth U.S. Circuit Court of Appeals, seated in New Orleans, studied my appeal.

This was a very trying time for my family. It seemed that we had been confronted with crisis and tragedy—earlier, the crushing realization that one of our daughters was retarded mentally; more recently, the death of our son. We had no monopoly on grief, but it did seem that we'd had our share.

While waiting for the appellate court's decision, I became embroiled in another political battle—one of the roughest, it turned out, of a career liberally punctuated with such controversies.

Questioned by the *Macon Telegraph's* political reporter while I was visiting the state capitol, I confirmed that I intended to pay my qualifying fee within the next few days to seek renomination in the Democratic primary election.

The announcement caused an immediate uproar. The Georgia Elections Code provided that any person convicted and "sentenced finally" for a felony is not eligible for office. I interpreted "sentenced finally" to mean that all appeals had to be exhausted.

The Bibb County Democratic Election Committee viewed the matter differently. Several days after my announcement the panel met behind closed doors in the offices of Phil Taylor, committee chairman. I appeared before the group briefly, stating my interpretation of the law.

Shortly after I left, the committee filed out and announced it had unanimously voted not to place my name on the September Democratic primary ballot.

Taylor explained to newsman that he and other members of the committee interpreted the state law as meaning that a person becomes ineligible to seek office at the time of sentencing for a felony offense, and can regain eligibility only by winning an appeal or gaining pardon.

I appealed the decision of the Bibb County Committee to the State Democratic Executive Subcommittee, which had final jurisdiction. On July 15, the subcommittee, after a closed door session in what was once the state Supreme Court chambers in the Capitol, overruled the Bibb Committee and directed that my name be placed on the September 11 primary ballot.

Taylor left the Capitol quickly after the decision was announced and declined to comment to newsmen; but another Bibb Democrat was ready to talk. The ruling, my fellow state representative, Mitch Miller, declared to reporters, was "political. It's poppycock. I don't think I could publicly be bound to support a criminal."

Taylor and the Bibb Democratic Executive Committee were not through. Three days later the panel unanimously adopted a resolution disassociating itself from my candidacy.

The move, according to Taylor, relieved other Democratic candidates from supporting me because of party loyalty.

Despite its antagonism towards me, the Bibb Democratic Committee was unable to talk any Democrat into running against me. (Keen was running in the Republican primary.)

In fact, a substantial number of Bibb Democrats had been circulating petitions promoting me as a write-in candidate in the event the local Democratic leadership succeeded in keeping my name off the ballot.

Keen also was unopposed in the Republican primary. As the primary election passed and the November general election approached, I threw myself into the activity of campaigning, trying to make it blot out the specter of the jail sentence hanging over my head.

When the returns were in, Keen had defeated me by a vote of 18,577 to 12,366.

As the days and weeks and then months dragged on after the election, and still no news arrived from the court in New Orleans, I was beginning to hope—unrealistically, of course—that "no news was good news." Sometimes I could almost make myself believe that we would never hear any more about my court case—that it was all just a bad dream that was now past and finished.

My wife, daughters, and I were at the supper table a

year after my election defeat when the telephone rang. It was the city editor of the *Macon Telegraph*.

"Bill, we just got the story of the appellate court upholding your perjury conviction, and I wanted to get your comment on it," the newsman said. "Are you going to appeal it further?"

After a moment's silence I replied that the phone call was the first I'd heard of the court's decision. I said I would withhold comment until receiving a copy of the ruling.

The Fifth Circuit Court issued its ruling on October 13, 1969, sixteen months after I had been convicted and filed notice of appeal.

When the phone call came, the court case was the last thing on my mind. The first few months after the appeal was filed, my family and I were constantly on edge, waiting to hear the outcome. But as time went on we thought about it less and less, although it still lurked, always, like an ogre in the background.

I had already made the tentative decision that the verdict of the Fifth Circuit Court would be final, as far as I was concerned. I had still had the option of appealing to the Supreme Court, but the case had been going on since 1965 and I had exhausted my financial resources. And the mental strain on me as well as my family had gone on long enough.

The appellate court said tersely, "The appellant has failed to demonstrate error in connection with his conviction."

The court had considered only one of the two counts on appeal, and my attorney has told me that this indicates they thought I was innocent on the other count. However, their verdict on the count dealing with overtime was controlling; and the chance that an appeals court might have thought me not guilty of the "turned-around room" count would prove little consolation when I was counting the days in prison.

My appeal on the overtime count was on the grounds that I did not use the same words in defining overtime as the three Macon workers later did.

"It is not necessary to prove the exact words of the accused in giving false statements," the Fifth Circuit Court said. It added that it was only necessary to "prove substantially what he said."

Shortly after learning the appellate court's ruling, I decided definitely that I would appeal the case no further.

That decision, of course, meant that I would go to prison.

I contend that my problems were basically political in origin, initiated not in Big Springs, Texas, but in my hometown of Macon, Georgia.

In general people are extremely reluctant to go into court unless they are forced to or unless someone makes it worth their while.

I believe considerable personal, business, and political influence was used to persuade the FHA to withhold the funds legally owed me and to pursue the case by seeking a criminal indictment. I base this largely on candid statements made to me by an FHA official at a cocktail party in Atlanta. After several drinks, he linked the original withholding of funds owed me by the FHA to an influential Macon citizen.

Little persuasion was needed to set the federal juggernaut in motion against me. As evidence, I cite the flat statement of the federal judge in my case that the Big Springs project was a "white elephant" and that the FHA needed a "goat."

16

JAIL LIFE is full of little surprises.

I was pacing up and down in the dayroom, from one end to the other, dragging a finger across the bars the way I used to drag a stick along a picket fence as a boy. I did that a lot—out of nervousness, out of boredom, out of a need to release pent-up energy. The other men in the dayroom spent most of the time sleeping, or fighting, or playing cards or dominoes, or trying to find a new form of all-male sex. I walked. Up and down, back and forth. I would have worn a path in the red-painted floor if I had stayed in that tank much longer.

I reached the end of the dayroom near the shower and toilet, daydreaming; it was one of the few times I almost forgot where I was. I turned to head back the other way, then I brushed against something and realized, with a start, that it was Charlie. He was nude, as usual. I instictively started to apologize; my only thought was that neither of us had seen the other. With his back to me, he was exerting steady pressure, jamming his buttocks hard into my stomach and groin, forcing me backward. I was suddenly pressed hard into the corner. I tried pushing against the back of his thick neck with both hands, but didn't even budge him. I felt him shoving harder as if he meant to squeeze my insides out.

Then Mike was looming in front of me, and I thought, "Oh my God, this is it." Mike, grinning and leering, reached over Charlie with arms crossed; he grabbed a bar on either side of my head, leaning in and he pressed both forearms hard into my throat. I was gasping for breath, fighting for my life.

Afterward I wondered what would have happened if Mike had held me there long enough for me to lose consciousness, or at least long enough to become too weak to defend myself. But now, the adrenalin flowing as it does in situations like this, giving me strength I didn't know I had, I managed to pull my knees up, push Charlie off me far enough to get one foot against his naked backside, and shove savagely and desperately. Charlie stumbled forward, almost tripped over Raymond's outstretched legs as the Negro sat impassively on the commode, then pitched forward into the shower stall and onto the floor.

Mike, his helpmate gone, perhaps fearful that Raymond had been aroused, immediately released his grip on the bars, took two quick steps backward, then moved casually back toward the other end of the dayroom. Charlie picked himself up off the floor, threw an arm around Mike's hairy shoulder, and walked with him. Neither of them even looked back at me. Not a word had been said. The other inmates sat or lay in their places, unmoving, just looking.

I stood there for a minute, rubbing my throat, trembling now that it was over, but relieved.

I thought, as I resumed my pacing, that perhaps now Mike would get off my back. Maybe I'd shown him I could take care of myself.

I was a dreamer. That was the day Mike finished making his knife.

He made it from a spoon. It took him several days to file it down, scraping it against a rough corner of the steel table. When he was through it had a point on the handle end of the spoon and two razor-sharp sides. I know how sharp they were, because Mike, with much fanfare, demonstrated by shaving the hair off an area of his left arm. He gathered everyone around him with the announcement: "C'mere and get a load of my new play-purty!"

He ran the knife down his arm, then shook the blade and the black hairs fell down to the floor.

From then on Mike used the knife like an extension of his own personality. It was always somewhere around him. He would sit at the table, sharpening it, sharpening it for what seemed like hours on end, often staring at me at the same time with a half-grin, half-sneer on his face.

Other times he would flip it around the room in an impossible game of mumblety-peg, dulling the blade against the metal and concrete, then sharpening it, sharpening it, all over again.

He would seem to dare me or anyone else to grab the knife. He left it laying around, or he tossed it in my direction. Once it bounced up against my pants leg, and I let it lay there until he ambled over. He picked it up, then stood there staring down at me, then he turned and walked away.

He sometimes used the knife to scrape paint off the bars and to scratch obscenities into the top of the table.

Once he went into the knife-fighter routine, standing in a half-crouch, tossing the knife from one hand to the other, muttering, whether to himself or to one of us, I couldn't tell: "All right, you bunch of sissies. Who's going to try to take me? Who's it gonna be? Doesn't nobody want to be a hero?"

He seemed to be in a half-trance, and I thought he was drugged. But I also wondered if he were crazy or getting that way fast.

David warned me against tangling with anyone who had a knife and knew how to use it. "I saw a guy scarred up bad with a knife just like that one," he said.

The warning really wasn't necessary.

Just after breakfast on my thirteenth day in jail, the

door to the dayroom opened. Over the speaker-system, a guard's voice echoed: "Latey—come on out."

At first I was surprised, then I was elated. This must mean they were finally ready to transfer me to a permanent prison. My spirits that morning had been very low. I'd been in the Tarrant County Jail now for almost two weeks, although the marshal who had brought me there had told me I could expect to be moved in a day or two. I'd had no contact at all with any jail officials other than guards, so I could only speculate as to the reasons for the long delay in transferring me.

I was beginning to wonder if I were going to have to serve my full sentence in this place, in day-to-day danger of a beating or homosexual attack. I didn't think my mind could stand much more of this pressure.

I jumped to my feet and hurried out. I could hear the low mumblings of the prisoners behind me; I knew they must be as curious as I was about what was going on.

"How long you been here, Latey?" the guard asked. "About a week, ain't it?"

"Two weeks."

"That right? Well, well. Time sure does fly when you're having a good time, don't it?"

We rode down the seven floors, separated by the bars in the elevator. Then the guard took me to the desk sergeant. The same U.S. marshal who had brought me here from the U.S. district court was standing there. I was delighted to see him but wanted to ask what took him so long.

175

"I've got some information for you, Laite," he told me. "The government wants you to be in Washington next Monday for a hearing."

"What do you mean?"

"Just what I said. Will you sign this to get out of this place?" He thrust a sheet of paper at me.

"I'll sign a contract with the devil himself to get out of here!" I told him, and he laughed.

"I don't know what's going on," he said. "I've never seen anything like this before, but I've been directed by the U.S. Bureau of Prisons to release you tomorrow, on your own recognizance, for a furlough, so you can attend this hearing. You have to sign this form today, so I can tell them you agree to do this and won't try to escape or leave the country. Then, after you leave Washington, you'll be transferred to another prison."

While he watched me, I glanced quickly over the form. I knew I must look strange to the marshal—different from the last time he'd seen me. I was unshaved, bleary-eyed from lack of sleep, still wearing the jail coveralls which now swallowed me up even more than they had originally because of all the weight I'd lost. And I knew I smelled like a skunk that had just been fished out of a cesspool.

I signed the paper, and the guard took me back to the elevator.

I was so overjoyed at the prospect of getting out the next day that I wanted to jump up and down and cheer. But I knew I was not out yet. I told myself that now I was going to have to curb my emotions even more than before. If Mike and the others guessed I was getting out the next day, there was no telling what they might try to do to me before I left.

As I got off the elevator on the seventh floor, I heard a commotion in the direction of my tank. As the doors clanged and I approached the entrance of the tank, accompanied by the same guard, the noise stopped.

The first thing I noticed as I stepped inside the dayroom was a new face. Another prisoner had been put in our tank. He was skinny and frail, but he had a fierce look on his face. He was standing just inside the door, hands on hips, glaring at the other inmates. His baggy prison shirt was dripping wet, and his hair was glistening, strands of it pasted down over his forehead.

The other prisoners were sitting around nonchalantly. I forgot about the new guy momentarily and mustered all my resources for one farewell performance. Despite my elation at the recent news, I forced myself to put on a glum face.

"So what's up, dude?" Mike asked. He was sitting beside Charlie on the table. Both of them were puffing cigarettes which I had rolled for David and which Mike had taken from him.

"Something about my mail," I muttered. "They said I'd been writing too many bad things and they were having to mark them out. They said I didn't know how lucky I was to be in this place."

For several long seconds Mike sat staring at me. I

couldn't guess whether or not he believed me. But apparently he did, because he started telling Charlie about a weekend in El Paso with two Mexican girls.

Then the new guy sounded off, and all our attention shifted to him.

He cut loose with a string of cuss words that would have embarrassed a drunken sailor, all the while shaking himself, sending drops of water flying in every direction. He reminded me of a Bantam rooster. He was cursing the other men and a good many branches of their family trees.

I held my breath and waited for the others to gang up on him and begin systematically breaking his bones. But they sat silent, and one or two of them were grinning.

My first thought when I'd seen the new man was that here was "fresh meat" for my depraved fellow inmates. I'd even wondered if perhaps they'd already attacked him, because he was obviously angry about something.

Apparently they'd had some fun with him, but it had been for them rather innocent fun. They'd punched him around a bit, and when he fought back and talked back instead of begging for mercy, they had dunked his head in the commode.

This hadn't fazed him, either. He was still boiling mad and raring to fight.

He stood there and pointed his bony finger at every man in the room in turn, including me, and dared each of us to take him on individually. His challenge to each man, repeated eight times (Raymond didn't even look up from his place on the commode; I wondered how they'd gotten him to move during the dunking) was approximately the same: "Come on, baby; you and me, baby; just you and me. If you've got any guts you'll try me, and I'll scatter your pieces all over the floor, baby. You'd rather tangle with a grizzly bear than tangle with me, baby."

Nobody took him up, although either Charlie or Mike could have lifted him with one hand and tossed him against the jail bars. It dawned on me that he had earned their respect by showing them he could be just as tough and mean and nasty as they were.

Finally he dismissed us all with a blanket description of our mothers' morals, and lay down to take a nap.

A few minutes later David eased over beside me. "He's something, isn't he?" David said. "Charlie and Mike and Richard held his head in the commode long enough to drown some people, and he came up fighting."

A minute later David changed the subject.

"You're getting out, aren't you?" he asked in a low voice.

"What makes you say that?" I asked, looking around to make sure we weren't being overhead. I didn't want to tell anyone, even David. I thought I could trust him, but I wasn't sure.

"It's just a feeling," he said. "I just wanted to tell you . . . I'm glad for you."

It was all I could do to keep my eyes dry.

The day dragged on with no more than the usual number of fights, arguments, and sex games. The other men kept their distance from the new man, though. I kept as far away from all of them as I could, praying silently for the night to come.

Eventually the new guy edged over near me and struck up a conversation. I suppose he had remembered that I'd been gone when he was dunked and couldn't have been in on it.

He asked me what I was in for, and I gave him the same line I'd given the others. Then he started singing the blues about his own hard times.

His name was Albert, and he couldn't have been more than eighteen years old. He had been picked up at a local night spot for drunkenness, he said, and he attributed an ugly gash on his forehead to a policeman's billy club. He said he'd had a headache ever since he got hit, two days before.

Finally the bell sounded to send us to our cells for the night—my last night there. I was walking on air.

I stepped into my cell. Then, just before the door slid shut, Albert stepped in with me.

I was startled and started to say something to him, but he sat down on one end of the bunk unconcerned about the whole thing, and I concluded that he must have been assigned to my cell while I was gone. All the other cells in the tank were occupied; apparently he would get mine after I left.

Meanwhile, I was more than a little irritated. It was my last night there, and I'd looked forward to relaxing in my cell and thinking ahead. Now there was a new complication.

I sat on the other end of the bunk. I didn't know what to say to the guy. I was inclined to be a little fearful about what he might try during the night, although I had no doubt that I could beat him if it came to that.

Albert suddenly jumped up and began shouting, trying to get the attention of a guard. "Hey, you guards," he yelled, throwing some descriptive adjectives. "What's going on? There are two of us in here!" He apparently thought there had been some mistake in the cell assignment; he didn't know I'd be leaving the next day.

His outburst set off the other prisoners. Their loud responses were predictable:

"Well, how nice! Why didn't one of us get to sleep with him?"

"You girls behave yourselves, now!"

"Some guys get all the luck. Save some for the rest of us!"

Albert let go with a few more choice examples of what he thought of them and then resumed his place on the end of the bunk.

We sat there, not looking at each other. I guess we were mentally debating whether we'd both try to sleep on the little bed or whether one would sleep on the floor, and if so, which one.

I started dominating the bunk. I did this by easing one foot, then the other, onto the bed, then extending them slowly in his direction.

He soon got the idea. He didn't make an issue of it. He just stood up, leaned against the bars of the door, smoked a cigarette, then lay down on the floor and rolled over underneath the bunk.

It was a weird feeling, knowing he was directly underneath me. I probably wouldn't have slept much anyhow, knowing I'd finally be leaving the Tarrant County Jail the next morning. But his presence made sure I would stay awake. I listened to every move he made. He seemed to toss around for at least an hour before dropping off into a snore-punctuated sleep.

I spent most of the night imagining the best and the worst that might happen after the hearing in Washington. I would picture myself in a marvelous new prison, where the inmates all had private suites and ate in carpeted, candle-lit dining rooms with linen napkins, fingerbowls, after-dinner drinks, and cigars. But when I finally fell asleep, I found myself in a dark, tank dungeon where the other prisoners had fangs and claws and the guards carried whips and butcher knives.

The next morning I was so excited I even ate the soggy toast and drank the stale coffee. Almost before I got it down, I heard footsteps coming down the hall and a guard bellowed, "All right, Latey—let's go!"

From my grin I'm sure the other men knew that I was leaving for good, but they only stared impassively as I prepared to leave. At the door I turned back to them. "You can have the money," I told them.

Almost four dollars of my original five was still piled

neatly on the floor where I had kept it the whole time. They were on it like dogs on a soupbone. Mike, I imagine, wound up with all of it.

Downstairs, I was given a form identifying me as a prisoner on furlough and was told to change back into my soiled, wrinkled suit. I had no driver's license, no social security card, no other identification of any kind.

The desk sergeant told me I could call my lawyer. The only phone I could use was a pay phone. I told the sergeant he'd have to lend me a dime, and he dug one out of his pocket. A guard left me at the phone. The operator put my call through to Bill Fonville's office in Dallas but the line was busy.

Then it occurred to me that I might call Marilyn. Why not? What could they do to me—put me in prison?

I placed the call collect to Macon. When it went through, my dime was returned.

"Marilyn . . . it's me." I found that my throat was tight, dry.

"Bill?" she answered. "Bill . . . what have you *done?* Have you broken out?"

It took me several minutes to assure her that everything was all right. I told her that I was about to fly to Washington and explained why. Then she gave me some news.

"Bill, you're going to be sent to Eglin Air Force Base. They've got a federal prison down there that sounds like it ought to be all right. It's an honor camp."

She said my attorney in Washington, who would be

handling my case at the hearing, had called her the day before and told her he had learned of the plans for my transfer.

I told her about my three-day furlough for the Washington trip. I said it would be great if she could meet me there, but I didn't know what the set-up there would be or whether it would be possible. Also, I didn't know if she could afford the trip.

She said she'd call my lawyer in Washington again and see what she could work out.

When I hung up, I tried Fonville's number again. I wanted him to arrange my plane ticket to Washington and wanted to fill him in on the latest developments. His phone was still tied up, so I called Bill Murphy in Dallas, the private investigator who had done some work for me during the course of the case. He said he'd have the ticket waiting for me at his office.

I went back to the desk sergeant. He returned the money they'd taken from me two weeks before—almost $100—and gave me a thick bundle of letters. They were letters I'd written and had thought were being mailed.

The desk sergeant said I'd been writing too much.

It seems the tale I'd told the other prisoners the day before had been a lot closer to the truth than I'd known.

The guard led me out the front door of the jail. Then, suddenly, I was on the street, alone. Free. At least for the time being.

I stood on the sidewalk, looking around me . . . at the buildings, the people . . . the sky and clouds . . .

the beautiful, lazy drift of smoke curling up from a factory smokestack . . . the sudden awareness of freedom was so overwhelming that I felt dizzied by it all. I felt a light, tingling sensation as I started to walk, almost as if my feet weren't quite touching the pavement. I was happy for the first time in two weeks.

"Thank you, Lord," I said aloud suddenly. A passing woman almost dropped her grocery bag.

I knew I must be enough to frighten anyone, even without shouting in the streets. More than anything else at the moment, I wanted a bath. I knew there was a hotel somewhere in this part of Fort Worth, but for the moment I couldn't get my bearings. When we'd entered the jail, fourteen days ago, it had been from another side, another level.

But then I turned a corner and spotted the hotel. I went in, ignoring the desk clerk's stares. Apparently he wasn't accustomed to such low class clientele.

In my room, I luxuriated in a very long, very hot shower. After that I went down to the hotel barber shop for a shave and haircut. A few minutes later, as the clerk stared even harder, I walked back through the lobby and called the hotel's limousine service to drive me to Bill Murphy's office in Dallas.

I picked up my tickets and boarded a jet for Washington.

As I relaxed on the plane, thinking of the paradox of my situation, I couldn't decide whether to laugh or cry, or both. The government, to keep possession of me, had seen fit to lock me up in a maximum security jail for two weeks. Now, for an interlude between the jail and permanent prison, they had, quite literally, set me free as a bird.

My attorney, Gaines Palmes, met me at the airport in Washington. He invited me to stay with him in his home in Alexandria, Virginia.

"There's somebody there you're going to be happy to see," he told me.

"Marilyn?"

"That's right."

She met us in the driveway. "Bill—you look terrible!" she cried. "But you look wonderful!" I knew what she meant.

Gaines and his wife left us alone, and for more than an hour we talked, and talked . . . about our girls, Marilyn's home life, my time in jail, about the transfer to Eglin. We were both optimistic about that.

The next morning Gaines and I drove to the hearing. It was held before the Board of Contract Appeals, an administrative panel that hears disputes involving various federal agencies.

At issue was some $30,000 to $40,000 still owed me on a job my firm had done for the Army at Fort Knox, Kentucky, converting duplexes into single-family homes. After my conviction in connection with the Big Springs, Texas, project, the government had been trying to avoid making payments on all my contracts. They didn't want to pay anything, not even for work that had been performed exactly as called for under the contract.

The hearing continued off and on for three days, and federal officials handling the Fort Knox project kept referring to my perjury conviction. Finally the chairman of the Board of Contract Appeals reprimanded the government for this. "Even if this man lied one time," he said caustically, "it doesn't mean he lies all the time."

Marilyn could only stay one night. Gaines and I drove her to the airport. It was hard to watch her board the plane and fly back out of my life. I couldn't know how long it might be before I would see her again.

The third day of the hearing, during a recess, I happened to pass a government file that had been left open on the hearing table. The letter on top had my name on it, and I stopped to look at it. I only had time for a quick glance before the federal officials started filing back in, but I got the gist of it.

It seemed the government felt if I were faced with having to come to Washington for the hearing as a prisoner, I might drop all claims against the FHA rather than suffer the humiliation involved.

It must have come as quite a shock for the government that I'd even shown up. If only they had known. Later, after the hearing had adjourned, I made it a point to tell one of the Army men how much I appreciated their bringing me to Washington. He was flabbergasted.

If they'd been smart, they'd have used exactly the reverse tactic. If they had only threatened to keep me in the Tarrant County Jail, I'd have gladly dropped every claim I ever had—or might ever have—against the government, and would have fawned shameless gratitude on them for giving me the opportunity.

In the end, no final decision was reached by the hearing board. As of this writing, the matter is still pending on appeal.

+   +   +

I had no idea what the procedure would be when I arrived at Eglin Air Force Base. How would they identify me? On the flight down, I remembered the nightmarish days in the Texas jail. I felt sure that the prison I was going to now would have to be an improvement.

At the terminal at Eglin, I stood uncertainly for a few minutes, not knowing what I should do. But then, an official-looking man in a gray-black uniform came up and asked me my name, then told me to come with him. It was midnight.

He handcuffed me before we got into the front of a pickup truck. We drove in silence to the prison compound. From his lapel badge, I saw that his last name was Henry. When we entered his office we found two prisoners asleep in chairs. He woke them.

Mr. Henry told me to strip and pack all my clothes in a box to be mailed home. The prisoners then directed me into a metal stall where one of them sprayed me with insecticide from a handgun. Then they led me to a shower.

Back in Mr. Henry's office, the two trusties issued me three sets of convict clothing—undershorts, undershirts, white socks, bluish-gray pants and shirts, a pair of brogans and a pair of regular shoes, plus a blanket, two sheets, a pillow case, toothbrush, a can of powdered toothpaste, shaving brush and a bar of soap.

They took my picture, profile and forward view, and gave me a number: 3759.

I was really a full-fledged prisoner now; I had my own number. They stenciled it on all my clothes, even on my underwear.

Another trusty came and gave me a card with my bed number and name. He took me to Barrack D and, with a flashlight, located my bunk. "You've got the upper," he said, and left me there.

It was dark. I couldn't see how to make up my bed. Also, I was afraid that if I tried, I might wake up the man in the lower bunk.

The place was so noisy, I didn't see how any of them could sleep. There was loud snoring, creaking bedsprings, sleep-talking peppered with profanities.

I looked around at the sleeping men, wondering how I would be accepted by them. I wondered what type of man was in the lower bunk under mine, and whether he or the prisoners in the bunks on either side of mine would be homosexuals or sadists.

After a few moments, I sighed and threw my things up on the top bunk. I climbed in as quietly as I could and lay there, wide-eyed, waiting for daylight.

17

IT DIDN'T TAKE ME LONG to realize just how reliable
a prison grapevine can be. The other prisoners in Barrack
D were talking about me almost before they got out of
bed my first morning there.

"Well, I see we got us that Georgia politician down
here," one of them said.

The reception was altogether different than the one
I'd received at the Tarrant County Jail. The other inmates
weren't cordial by any means, but at least they weren't
openly hostile.

The prison at Eglin Air Force Base, in the Florida
panhandle about forty miles east of Pensacola, is an
honor camp. There are no prison walls and no bars on the
windows, but discipline is strict. Guards patrol the prison
area constantly, and there is regular counting and check-
ing of inmates, both day and night.

The inmates include many of the white-collar type, but there are also many hard-core prisoners who have been transferred from maximum security units shortly before being released. These prisoners do the hard labor at the Air Force Base. The white-collar prisoners handle various administrative chores at the base.

The prison population of about 430 included 30 lawyers—the "Wall Street Corporate Counsels," I called them. There were five bank presidents, the president of a life insurance company, and a sheriff from Tennessee. There was also a Catholic priest from Miami. He was in for harboring an alien, his nephew from Cuba.

+   +   +

I had not slept from the time I crept up into my bunk at about 2 a.m. until a trusty came into the barracks about 5 a.m., turned on the lights, and let loose a blast on his whistle to rouse everyone out of bed.

The prisoner in the bunk under mine turned out to be from Buena Vista, Georgia, a little town not far from Macon. He was serving time on a bootlegging charge, he told me. His name was Randall.

I rolled up my baggy prison trousers and followed him and the others to the dining room for breakfast. I noticed that most of the other men appeared to have clothes that fit rather well. I remembered that the trusty who had guided me to the barracks the night before had told me I should have my pants and shirt altered.

That first day at Eglin was a Sunday, and there was no organized activity except for meals and regular head-counts. I tried to be friendly, in hopes the others in the barracks would do the same, but was disappointed when most of them failed even to acknowledge my greetings.

Nevertheless, I commented in a letter to Marilyn: "There is no comparison between this place and where I was. This place is a compliment to the prison system. You are treated like a human being here."

But the next day I began to wonder if I had spoken too soon. I was taken, along with seven other new prisoners, to the Air Force Base hospital for X-rays. The Air Force medic who was conducting the X-rays wanted all eight of us to stay in the room while each was exposed separately. This meant each of us would be exposed to the X-rays eight times, and although I wasn't at all sure, it sounded dangerous to me. I vaguely remembered reading articles by doctors warning of the dangers of too much X-ray exposure to patients.

I asked if I could wait outside until my turn came. "Hell no, you lousy convict!" the medic snarled. "What are you—some kind of trouble maker?"

Before I could try to explain or reason with him, he called a trusty who shepherded me to a prison administrator. There I was given a stern lecture on the necessity of obeying orders without question. "When you're told to do something, by God you do it—no matter if it's bad for your health or what!" the administrator told me; then added, "Just because you've got a college education, don't think that means a hill of beans to us!"

I didn't understand what he meant by that, unless he thought I might be considering exerting some leadership among the other prisoners in seeking fair treatment.

Nevertheless, I was X-rayed several days later—alone.

+   +   +

Gradually I began learning the prison routine; but I had to learn everything the hard way. Nobody told anyone anything. Often I thought of the plea of a freshman Bibb County legislator during a particularly confusing instance of parliamentary maneuvering in the House: "I want to do right, really I do . . . but I'm just a little confused. . . ."

In prison, no one takes the trouble to straighten you out.

I was on hard labor details my first two weeks at Eglin. We went out on trucks in the mornings, worked at digging and cutting grass along the roadsides, and came back at night exhausted and sweaty and dirty. Pretty soon too many of my suits were in the laundry, and the one I had on was getting stiff enough to stand by itself. I couldn't understand why the laundry hadn't sent back my clothes, because I'd seen them bring Randall's back to his bin a day or two after he'd sent them out. But when I asked him if he knew what the problem was, he only grunted.

Then, finally, he told me. "Listen, you'd better wise up and start leaving the laundry men some cigarettes."

The trusty who did the laundry, Randall said, required payment of a carton of cigarettes a month. Prisoners who didn't pay off didn't get their clothes back.

There was an area in the laundry where a prison official issued emergency clothes. I went there and told the official that I was desperate for some clean clothes. He must have seen from the condition of those I was wearing that I was telling the truth, because he gave me two ragged sets of pants and shirts.

As I was leaving the laundry, two prisoners stopped me in the hallway. "What were you doing in there?" one of them asked. I didn't like their manner, or the way they were pressing in on me from both sides.

I explained why I'd had to ask for emergency clothes.

"Did you tell him why you didn't get your other clothes back?" the other one asked.

"If you're talking about the cigarettes—no I didn't."

"All right then. If you want your clothes back from now on, buddy, you'd better start leaving those cigarettes where they're supposed to be. Everyone will stay a lot happier and healthier that way."

With that they turned and walked away. I was pretty well shaken-up because, although I wasn't really sure, I thought I'd just been threatened.

+ + +

I soon learned that a carton of cigarettes was the

going rate for getting clothes altered, too. I hadn't had a chance to go to the commissary to buy any cigarettes, so I shortened the legs of my remaining pair of pants myself. Then, when they came back from the laundry (by then I'd bought cigarettes and left a carton for the laundry man) the pants had shrunk so that they barely reached below my knees.

+   +   +

As the days passed I came to realize that cigarettes are the basic medium of exchange in prison, just as money is on the outside. None of the services that trusties are supposed to perform for other prisoners would ever get done if the trusty's palm was not crossed with cigarettes.

Gambling was strictly outlawed but still it went on all the time, and the stakes were usually cigarettes.

Drugs and whiskey were plentiful, and again most convicts paid for them in cigarettes.

The barber had to be paid a carton a month. Otherwise, you'd get in the chair, he'd give you three quick spins—and that was it. Then the guards would get on your back for not having a fresh haircut.

The mailman had to be paid a carton a month to deliver mail. Extra packs of cigarettes would buy special deserts at mealtimes, starch in your shirts, or new soles on your shoes.

Some of the degenerates in the prison paid with cigarettes to have homosexual acts performed on them or to be allowed to perform certain acts on others.

We were each given a $20-a-month account to spend in the commissary. This money is furnished by your family; you can spend that much but no more. During my stint at Eglin, it took all my $20 each month for cigarettes—and I don't even smoke.

I learned quickly that, honor camp or no honor camp, these weren't Boy Scouts I was living with. There was tension in the air at all times, and the danger of an incident suddenly exploding into violence was always present.

+   +   +

My first visitor at Eglin was a Department of Housing and Urban Development investigator, R. R. Renschi. I had no idea what he wanted, and he seemed in no hurry to tell me. He began by talking about how he was having problems with his young son, and how sorry he was that mine had been killed. Gradually, though, I recognized that he was trying to get me started talking about jobs my company had done for the government.

My prison parole officer, Mr. Foley, kept interrupting and telling him he had to advise me of my legal rights. He told Renschi this three times without any results. Finally Foley himself told me that any information I gave Renschi could be used against me in court.

At that time I told the HUD investigator that if the government wanted any more information from me, they would have to subpoena it, and that I would not talk to him any longer without my attorney present.

This perturbed him, and he admitted that the government wasn't satisfied with the disposal of my case. "We think Judge Brewster was much too lenient with you," he said. The government was considering seeking another indictment against me for submitting false statements saying that bills were paid when it had evidence that they weren't paid, he added.

I later received affidavits from five leading contractors in Macon confirming that I had paid the bills in a manner that was both legal and customary. The government never sought the indictment.

The inmates at Eglin were on the lookout for any activity to pass the long hours. I found that the less you have to do with other prisoners, the better off you are. This was against my nature, but it worked. I walked a lot, mostly around an open field. I did anything I could to stay busy, because those who sat around talking seemed invariably to wind up in a scrap or some sort of trouble. One day during my second week there, an older prisoner who had been friendly to me, a jewel thief named Harry Sitner, told me Lou Wolfson wanted me to meet him out at the athletic field.

I recalled that Louis E. Wolfson was the millionaire who received a good deal of publicity for his connection with the Abe Fortas case. Fortas resigned his seat on the Supreme Court after it was revealed that he had accepted $20,000 as a consultant to the Wolfson Family Foundation in 1966, though he had returned it a year later. Wolfson served nine months at Eglin. He had been convicted of violation of securities laws. Of course, this had nothing to do with Fortas.

After my conviction and before I went to prison I had read that Wolfson was serving a sentence and was imprisoned at Eglin. I had written him, mentioning that I was in somewhat similar circumstances but did not yet know where I would serve my time.

His secretary had answered my letter, and she had apparently written Wolfson about it.

He and I began taking daily walks around the athletic field together. We had a few things in common. Our financial standing was not one of them. Firstly, he was interested in politics. He, like me, had attended the University of Georgia, on a football scholarship. One year he had given every member of the graduating class some stock in his corporation. Both of us were extremely concerned about the need for prison reform.

Wolfson seemed compassionate, and very concerned about inequities in the judicial system and the possible influence of organized crime on the judicial branch of government. He felt that some judges were being controlled by the Mafia; he favored some sort of recall system whereby unsatisfactory judges could be voted out of office.

He was bitter about his own case. He had asked his judge to postpone sentencing because of the serious illness of his wife. The judge had refused, and while Wolfson was being sentenced, his wife had died.

Wolfson was also very concerned about repeaters. It

discouraged him that so many prisoners at Eglin had been out and then returned one or more times. "You can't even make a dog do tricks unless you reward him," he once told me. "The prison system as it is now is creating hardened criminals rather than rehabilitating them."

If a prisoner were allowed to earn money in prison, he maintained, this would serve a double purpose: It would serve as a reward at the time it was earned, and it would help the man build up a nest egg to start a new life when he was free.

After my two weeks of hard labor, I was assigned to the prison's education department, interviewing and testing incoming prisoners. Wolfson also worked there, and I was being groomed to take over his job when he was released the latter part of January.

I'm convinced that Wolfson headed off a number of escapes. He always found time to listen to other convicts who had serious problems. Many men turned to him for advice rather than to the prison counselor.

18

UNDER THE TYPE OF SENTENCE given to me by
Judge Brewster, I was eligible to apply for parole immediately. But Eglin had a rule. If you hadn't entered the
prison by the 10th of November, you couldn't appear before the December meeting of the parole board. And the
board didn't return until February.

I had entered Eglin November 29th, so that meant I
was stuck there until at least sometime in February.

My routine at Eglin was generally as follows: Rise at
5 a.m., sweep and mop around bunk, then line up for
breakfast; at 7:30 a.m. report to control center to be
counted, then report to education department; 11 a.m.,
eat lunch, return to work; 3:30, be counted again; 4:00,
supper.

I was getting mail regularly from Marilyn, Kelly, and
Jenny. New prisoners were allowed to receive mail only

from three persons on an approved list, and of course I had selected my wife and girls. As a prisoner built up good days, he might be allowed to expand his mailing list. I expanded mine by slipping the mailman a carton of cigarettes once a month; after I learned that trick, he'd bring me mail from anyone.

When I first arrived at Eglin I was, as the other prisoners called it, "quarantined." During this period of isolation, or probation, new prisoners were not allowed to communicate with their families at all. This apparently is meant to indoctrinate a new prisoner; to make him realize just how cut off from the rest of the world he really is; how helpless he is. Then it is assumed that he will adopt the proper attitude of subservience.

Even during the "quarantine" period, however, the prison authorities can't prevent an inmate from writing to his trial judge, his congressman, or the U.S. Attorney General. And the prison was prohibited from censoring such letters.

Rather cleverly, I thought, I sent a letter to U.S. Senator Richard Russell, enclosing a letter to Marilyn and asking Russell's office to forward it.

A few weeks later I found out that my plan hadn't been so original after all. With every uncensored letter mailed by a quarantined prisoner, the prison sent along a note that read something like this: "If the writer has enclosed mail to anyone other than the addressee and asked you to forward it, you will please disregard such request and return the unauthorized mail to Eglin AFB Prison."

Fortunately for me, Senator Russell's office had disregarded the note and sent my letter on to Marilyn.

The food was fairly good at Eglin. On Friday nights we had pie and on Sunday nights ice cream. The men looked forward to those two nights each week the way a kid looks forward to Christmas.

We had our only taste of steak at Eglin one night when formal ceremonies were being held. High-ranking prison officials were visiting, so at the last minute, the menu was changed from meatloaf to steak.

Convicts aren't supposed to have any food or drinks in the barracks. But ingenuity prevailed. The men liked to have that one last cup of coffee in the morning after breakfast, before leaving for work. They'd take a metal trash can and fill it about half full of water. Using a special kind of wire one of them had made, they'd stick one end of it in an outlet and the other end in the water. As soon as the water was hot, there was plenty of instant coffee for everyone in the barrack.

If a guard happened to come through, several inmates would gather around the trash can, propping their feet on it and engaging in animated conversation until the guard had passed.

Harry Sitner was one of the few bright spots in the dreary prison life. Harry was referred to as "the international jewel thief" and perhaps he was. I never heard him talk about any international jewel thievery, but I often listened to him gleefully describe how he had fleeced wealthy racing fans by stripping their motel rooms while they attended the Kentucky Derby. "But one thing I never did," he always added, "I never took nothing from the poor, only from the rich."

Harry Sitner was seventy-four years old, and he had spent thirty-five of those years in prison. He was a little, gray, wiry wisp of a man. He always wore an oversized coat, and it was always loaded down with contraband—inevitably including a sack of prunes which he offered to all he met. In a place where almost everyone else was trying to take advantage of you in one way or another, that was true kindness, albeit an unusual sort.

He was always doing little favors for other prisoners, usually anonymously. A new prisoner would come in without any commissary money and no likelihood of any, and Harry would arrange with some of his prison friends to have some money put in the new man's commissary account. Or a prisoner who was especially down on his luck would pull down his bed covers at night and there would be candy, fruit, or some other small gift, courtesy of Harry Sitner.

Harry didn't have much to look forward to on the outside, assuming a man his age could live long enough to ever see the outside again. His wife was blind. His son had changed his name because he didn't want to be linked to his convict father. But any man at Eglin AFB prison would have mortgaged a piece of his soul—if there was an unmortgaged piece left—for Harry Sitner, international jewel thief, universal humanitarian.

One of the most moving experiences of my prison

term took place about a week before Christmas. The Eglin Air Force Base Women's Auxiliary marched to the front of the barracks one night and sang Christmas carols for us.

They were brave women. Many of the men crowding around the barracks windows had not seen a woman for months and had not touched one for much longer than that. There were no bars between us and them. I had seen some of the same men almost go berserk when they were working on a road detail and a woman merely drove past them.

But on this night, music soothed the savage beasts. By the time the women left, there were few dry eyes in the barracks. They had shown us simple human kindness. They had shown us that somebody cared after all—and that, for many of the convicts, was a rare expression indeed.

That night, the prison superintendent passed through the barrack, handing out sacks of hard candy and soft drinks to all the men.

This was, without doubt, the worst loneliness of my whole prison sentence. To be separated from wife and family at this special and meaningful time of year is bad enough. To be away from them, and wearing the garb of a convict, is mental anguish of the worst sort.

At Eglin I found there were prisoners with special talents. One was Bob Davidson who worked with me in the education department. He was a very likable guy; short, with prematurely gray hair cut in a crewcut. Most of his life had been spent in either juvenile or adult prison institutions. He had learned all the angles. No matter what he did, no matter how strange it seemed at the time, he had a good, logical reason for doing it. Sooner or later the results would benefit Bob Davidson.

One day in early December, I decided to stay in the education department at noon to take care of some extra work. I notified the control center that I would not be going to the dining room.

While I was sitting alone at my desk, the door opened and in walked Bob with a little guy everyone called Weasel—because, I suppose, he looked like one. They stopped cold, just inside the door, staring at me.

"Hello, Bob," I said. "What's up?" Neither of them said a word.

Then Bob closed the office door and locked it. The two of them moved a heavy filing cabinet against the door. Still without having spoken a word to me, they took small tools from their pockets and began carefully removing paneling from the wall. They opened a hole about two feet square. I could see a rope hanging down in the hole. First Weasel, then Bob squeezed through the hole and slid down the rope.

About ten minutes later they came back up. Each pulled out a hot water bottle from under his shirt. From the odor, I knew the rubber bottles contained moonshine.

The two were operating a still, right under the education office. The still must have been hooked up to the boiler that heated the building.

Bob took a small wrench out of his shoetop and loosened the end of a pipe that ran along the wall. Then both emptied the hot water bottles into the pipes. They fastened the paneling back to the wall, returned the cabinet to its place, and left the room, still without ever acknowledging my presence.

I sat there dumbfounded. In a few minutes I got up, examined the end of the pipe, and found it was a dummy. It had no real function. Inside the building, it ended in a corner. The other end curved into the wall. I looked out a window and saw that the pipe extended just outside the building. Bob and Weasel would, no doubt, slip back over to the building that night and help themselves to whiskey out of the pipe.

A minute later, another prisoner, whom I'd seen hanging around with Weasel off and on, came in with a mop and bucket of pine oil. He mopped the floor three times, using plenty of pine oil. By the time he'd finished, no one would be able to sniff out any trace of moonshine.

Three days later word came over the intercom for me to report to the prison's assistant superintendent. The civilian supervisor of the education department, Mr. Russmisell, remarked, "You hear that, Laite? What trouble have you gotten into?"

As two guards drove up to the door to pick me up, Bob Davidson glared at me.

When I arrived at the administration building, I was met outside the door by the assistant prison superintendent, Mr. Cancellor. "How's it going, Laite?" he asked, in what seemed to be a friendly enough tone.

"Fine, sir."

"Let's go inside."

I was in a turmoil. The only thing I could figure was that word of the moonshine still had somehow leaked to the prison authorities, and they'd connected me with it. If this was true, I could be a two-time loser. My chances for parole could be spoiled, and if Bob Davidson was linked to the still, he'd figure me for a stoolie and be out for revenge.

Cancellor sat down in the chair at his desk, his back to me, feet propped on a window sill. I stood nervously before the desk.

"Laite . . . you got any whiskey?"

"No, sir."

"Do you drink whiskey, Laite?"

"Yes sir. If I were home, I'd like to have a little drink now and then."

"Do you drink any whiskey in here?"

"No, sir, I don't."

"Well, you're in here for lying, aren't you? Do you expect me to believe you?"

"I don't know who told you I was drinking, but he's the one that's lying. And I'd like to tell him that to his face," I said. Some of my nervousness had begun turning to anger.

"You won't get a chance to do that. Coleman Clark

told me. But we caught him stealing in the commissary, and he's been sent back to the Atlanta Pen."

"Well, he's the one that's lying this time."

"He said he knew you on the outside."

"That's not true, either. I knew he was from Blakely, Georgia, but that's all I knew about him. I never saw him before I came in here."

"All right, Laite. If you see any whiskey, will you tell me?"

"No, sir."

At that moment he swung around in his chair to face me.

"Oh, in other words, you'd lie to me about it?"

"No, sir. If you ask me a direct question about some specific whiskey, I'll answer you truthfully. But I don't think it's my obligation to come in here and volunteer any information like that. I try to tend to my business and do my time."

"Okay, Laite, that's fair enough. You're free to return to your job assignment."

I walked back to the education department, worrying all the way that Bob Davidson would think I squealed.

I'd heard before about how prisoners in trouble would try to shift the blame to another man or try to get a fellow con in trouble with the officials just for the hell of it. That's apparently what Coleman Clark had done.

When I returned to the education department I found Bob Davidson waiting, sitting on a corner of his desk. We stared at each other without saying anything.

The subject didn't come to the surface between us until some two weeks later, just before Davidson was to be released. One day I told him, "Bob, do you have any idea what kind of pressure you and Weasel put me under that day?"

"Yeah, I do," he said. "But in the first place, you weren't supposed to be there. And in the second place, we couldn't change our plans. We knew we had to take a chance. And we knew that if you told, we'd find out about it. You're a healthy man today because you kept your mouth shut."

Then he grinned. "Hell, come on, shake on it. Tell you what, come on down to my bunk and I'll let you listen to some music with me."

I didn't know what he was talking about. We were not allowed to have any radios or phonographs in prison.

He showed me his set-up. In the education department were several tape recorders. He'd run a wire all the way from there to the barrack and inside to his bunk, where it was hooked up to earphones. The tape recorder would play silently for hours into the night after Davidson left the office each day. Back snug in his barrack bunk, he'd slip on the earphones and listen to music until he fell asleep.

The time passes slowly when you're in prison, even when you have a fairly decent job as I had in the education department. The monotony of the work, the knowledge that you're locked up, the absence of friends and loved ones, the constant threat of violence or homosexual attack—all seem to stretch the days and weeks out in an endless line before you.

I had plenty of time to daydream. Mostly, I thought of Marilyn and the girls, Jenny and Kelly. The daily activities that I'd always taken for granted in life . . . sitting down to breakfast with two sleepy-headed girls and their always wide-awake mother . . . helping little Kelly with her arithmetic . . . coming home tired from work to find two highballs sitting there, waiting . . . all these things seemed so much more important now that I no longer had them.

Late at night I'd lie in my prison bunk and think how great it would be to be able to walk out into the kitchen and raid the refrigerator.

At work in the education department, I would almost physically ache with longing to pick up the telephone, call someone, anyone, just to chat with a friend.

Reading the daily paper, watching the news on television . . . drinking from a glass instead of a paper cup or from a fountain . . . taking a bath with a real bar of soap instead of the liquid kind . . . sleeping a whole night without a guard flashing a light in my face . . . some pleasant conversation during a meal . . . a little simple privacy—all these came to seem like the most marvelous of luxuries, worthy of conscious enjoyment rather than routine acceptance.

Your mind can start to play tricks on you as the weeks in prison wear on. I began to have nagging doubts about how important I really was to my family. Were they getting along just as well without me? Did they really miss me? How were they taking what had happened to me?

But I realized at other times, when I was somethat out of the doldrums and thinking more rationally, that my family might be getting the worst of it. They had to stay there in Macon and bear the stigma of my prison sentence. In some ways, that was worse than having to serve the sentence. At least I was isolated from the social repercussions of my conviction.

As much as I disliked my condition, I knew that many of my fellow inmates were much worse off than I. I had the support of my family. Many of the other convicts had no one on the outside who cared what happened to them. For many of them, the first mail they received in prison was a "Dear John" letter from a wife or girlfriend.

Some had extra burdens to bear, coming to prison on drug charges or as alcoholics. They had the weight of those habits to add to the other pain and suffering of prison life. They received no sympathy from anyone as they sweated out the agonies of withdrawal.

Marilyn and I had begun making plans for her to visit me about the first of the year. It had not been as simple a decision as one might think. I had said very firmly that I did not want the children to come. They were at impressionable ages; I didn't want them to see me in my convict's uniform and didn't want them exposed to the prison atmosphere.

My wife put her foot down. They all wanted to see me, and they were all coming.

But the days dragged by as I waited for the day when they would come.

19

ONE DAY AFTER I had been at Eglin about a month, I was stopped on the grounds by a prison official who knew me by name. He asked me to go to a certain barrack to locate a certain Negro prisoner.

I entered the barrack and saw several white convicts sitting on the floor playing cards. I asked one of them if he had seen the man, whose name was Nolan, and the inmate asked whether Nolan was white.

"No," I said. "He's a Negro."

The next thing I knew a powerful arm was circling my neck, yanking my head back; sharp steel was touching my throat. He held me helpless, the point of his knife at the hollow of my throat, while he held my right arm twisted up behind me in a hammerlock. "What did you say, whitey?" His breath was hot against my ear.

By that time I was straining up on my toes from the pressure of the knifepoint. "I said, 'Negro,'" I said, enunciating the word carefully, thinking perhaps I had slurred it before.

"Uh-uh, whitey. You don't call us Negroes—you call us blacks."

"Yes, sir," I grunted, and a second later he released me, turned, and walked out of the building without looking back.

I went back and told the prison official he would have to get somebody else to go find Nolan for him.

The mental strain was less at Eglin than at the Tarrant County Jail partly because my mind had become conditioned to the constant threat of physical abuse.

At Eglin I saw no forced homosexuality, such as I had witnessed at the Texas jail, but there was a great deal of homosexuality between consenting individuals.

In fact, during my first few weeks there, homosexuality seemed to be extremely widespread. But after I'd been there awhile I became hardened to it; and I began to notice it only occasionally.

One reason it seemed so widespread at first was that the homosexuals always made it a point to "check out" every new man. I was no exception. They had their technique honed to near perfection: the nonchalant pat on the behind as you walked along together, the comrade-like draping of an arm over your shoulder, a casual hand on your knee as you sat in the darkened movie, flattering comments on your muscular build. They went only far enough to let you know what was available if you were interested but never quite far enough to openly antagonize you if you weren't.

Eventually I learned who made up the hard-core group. They stayed close together, exchanging favors within the group, while always keeping an eye out for any available extracurricular activities as well.

Sometimes when two or three of them were standing around together, you could hear them talking—about you or another possible candidate for conquest. "Old Bill there, he won't be seeing little wife for a long time," one might say, eyeing me casually.

"Yeah, that's right. I'll just bet he's hurting real bad too. Something tells me he'll be coming around before long."

If you ignored them, they'd usually move on, looking for someone more acquiescent.

Though I saw no actual assaults at Eglin, the danger, the potential, was always there. And in spite of popular stereotypes, some of the biggest, meanest, roughest men at Eglin were members of the hard-core "homo" clan.

Most of the homosexuality I stumbled across was in the showers. In the barrack there was one big shower room with several nozzles, and six or eight men would gather in there at the same time. I soon learned to take my baths before or after the main group took theirs—whenever possible, during the times when I knew the guards would be making their rounds.

A laundry bin on wheels stayed next to the showers. It was usually half full of dirty clothes. One morning as I passed it I saw that it was shaking, rather violently, and some unusual sounds were coming from inside it. I looked in. There were two men in there, partially hidden under the dirty laundry. As I walked away the bin was still shaking. They had not noticed my presence.

There was sometimes a link between homosexuality and other bodily cravings. After their money was exhausted, alcoholics or drug addicts would turn to performing homosexual acts on others to obtain a drink or a fix.

The addicts were among the most pitiful men in prison. Many of them could obtain only enough drugs to keep them on the habit; most of the time they were in a state of trembling need, then frenzied despair, their bodies completely out of their control. Then they became the absolute slaves of the peddlers of dope, willing to do almost literally anything to satisfy their physical and mental longing.

Several times a month a prisoner would be shipped out after being caught using or pushing drugs. One of the men who worked in the infirmary smuggled some of the narcotics and syringes into the barracks. Other drugs were brought into the camp by visitors.

Tension was always in the air at Eglin, and although there was relatively little open violence, there always seemed to be a fight hanging there, just looking for an excuse to happen. Guards were little help in protecting the inmates' safety. I had been warned early by other prisoners not to speak to a guard unless he spoke to me first. "Your first loyalty is to the other prisoners," another prisoner had told me. "Remember that. You don't hear anything, you don't see anything—and you damn sure don't tell anything."

After awhile, you don't worry about being killed in prison, but nonetheless a nagging fear is always present. There is no way to be prepared for every eventuality. You have to condition yourself, keep reminding yourself that you're existing in a foreign environment, and that almost every other man in that environment is your enemy. And your enemies know that environment better than you; they're experienced in all the subtle, unwritten rules of survival there. So if you're going to make it, if you're going to find your way through the maze and come out the other end in one piece, you've got to keep alert every minute, night and day. You can never afford to relax even for a few seconds.

In prison a man's life may be worth no more than a nickel candy bar or a $2 carton of cigarettes. I've seen contracts taken out on other inmates to have them beaten in varying degrees. For two packs of cigarettes, a thug might break your arm. For four packs, he'd break an arm and close both your eyes. For a carton, he'd kill you.

Many prisoners look forward to the arrival of a new man because they can always count on having a little fun with him. The inmates have their own rules, and they are rigidly enforced. A newcomer has no way of knowing what the rules are, of course, and everyone is careful not to tell him. But let him innocently break one, no matter how small, and punishment is swift and certain. Each cellblock at Eglin had a disciplinary unit. Black prisoners punished black offenders, and white prisoners punished white offenders.

One rule at Eglin concerned the television set in the recreation room. Selecting the channel was the prerogative of the senior prisoner, from the standpoint of time served. Protocol required that any other prisoner check with him before changing the station, even if the prisoner was the only man in the recreation room at the time.

Violators of this rule were punished by the other men, just as other violators were punished for breaking in line, stealing, squealing to a guard, or any other action not considered in the best interest of the other prisoners.

The veteran prisoners are a particularly clever and conniving bunch; they've got something going all the time. They're always on the lookout for a new adventure, a new pigeon, a new form of violence or sex to break the grinding monotony.

Wolfson warned me early not to discuss my family, my business, or anything else about my life on the outside with any prisoner. They were always looking, he said, for any scrap of information that could be used to their advantage when they got out, often in the form of blackmail.

"Keep in mind," he told me, "that some of them will be getting out before you do. You don't want them looking up your family or your friends while you're stuck down here."

One new prisoner at Eglin, a short, chunky redhead called Cooter, came into the place fighting. The first man who looked askance at him, Cooter jumped on with both feet. Ditto the second and the third. After a few days Cooter was black and blue and bloody, but he had plenty of company. Finally someone asked him what was bothering him.

"Listen, I've been in prison before," Cooter said. "I knew everybody in here would be just waiting to see me get in a fight, so I figured there was no sense in keeping them waiting."

The old heads in prison are always looking for a chance to set up a new guy for a fall, solely to have the fun of watching him topple. He'll be standing right there with his hand in the cookie jar right up to the elbow when the guards arrive—and the old timers will be nowhere in sight.

They'll place contraband—liquor, drugs, weapons— in your bed or locker when they know a shakedown is coming, then sit back innocently and wait for the fun to start. I learned early in the game to search my own area regularly to get rid of such plants before the guards arrived.

You're always trying to build up "good days" in prison. At Eglin six good days are deducted from your sentence for every month served. On a year's sentence, for example, a prisoner who lost none of his good days would be released seventy-two days early, even if he were not paroled. The old timers derived great satisfaction from spoiling the good days of another prisoner who had only a short time remaining on his sentence, or one who came in with only a few months to serve. If a guard found a bottle of whiskey in your locker, all the good days you'd built up might be erased. The major threat the prison held over inmates to enforce discipline was the revocation of good days, that and transferral to a maximum security unit.

Prisoners with short sentences always seem to irritate the old timers. "You came in here with a damn parole," they tell such prisoners.

Social status in prison is sharply pronounced. The worse the crime, the higher the rank. Any crime of violence or any crime involving firearms ranks high on the ladder. So does any crime that requires a great degree of courage—extortion was included in this category.

Perjury was on the bottom rung. Just a notch above that was draft dodging, and violation of the white slave traffic act (transporting females across state lines for immoral purposes) was only slightly higher.

The important thing to remember about the social order was that the ones on the bottom end were supposed to obey the orders of those on the top.

Verbal harrassment, to a greater or lesser degree, went on all the time. The prisoners created a fictitious "Jodie," a name denoting a stranger who would move in and fill in for a prisoner after he left home.

"What you reckon the little woman's doin' tonight?" one prisoner would ask another. "You reckon ol' Jodie's takin' care of her?"

If you had even the slightest tendency toward jealousy, they could drive you almost insane.

I often saw a man refused medical attention when it seemed obvious to me that he was badly in need of it. This apparently was the price the really sick prisoners had to pay for the dozens of malingerers. So many men attempted to get out of work assignments—or even get themselves discharged from prison—for phony health reasons that the prison officials were naturally skeptical. But though that may be a reason, it is not an excuse for allowing sick men to suffer needlessly.

In the infirmary, men were deliberately mistreated and humiliated to discourage them from returning. Over and over they were warned that if they stepped out of line they could be sent from the honor camp to some place like the Atlanta Pen or Fort Leavenworth.

I got to know a prisoner named Gene pretty well. He came to Eglin a day before me; he was No. 3758 and I was 3759. He was from Atlanta, serving a term for interstate transportation of stolen securities.

By a freak coincidence, he had been on the third floor of the Tarrant County Jail about the same time I was on the seventh floor. He had been in the tank with Johnny Ray Smith, the prisoner who had been sentenced by Judge Brewster just before me. Gene told me Smith had mentioned being in the courtroom with a defendant from Macon.

Gene constantly complained about not feeling well, and about not being able to get anything done for him in the infirmary. He was released on February 12. On February 17, he died. I heard about his death through the prison grapevine and was later able to verify it.

Even if a man succeeded in getting treatment in the infirmary, it is questionable how much he would be helped. Convicts with nothing but a little on-the-job training gave the shots, handed out pills, and performed most of the treatment.

Rather than watch the cartoons on television—that was the usual fare—I took courses in philosophy and comparative religion at a nearby junior college two nights a week.

Visitors were allowed at the prison on Saturdays, Sundays, and holidays. Marilyn and the children planned to come for a visit on New Year's Day.

Having visitors was like getting mail; each visitor had to be approved by prison officials prior to a visit. If the prison hadn't gotten around to approving someone, he was turned away at the gate, even if he'd driven hundreds of miles.

An outdoor area for visiting was separated by a wire fence from the rest of the prison. It included tables and benches, and many visiting families would bring along picnic lunches.

A guard manned a desk at the entrance to the visiting

area, and guards and trusties patrolled inside. The prisoners were searched before entering or leaving the area, but visitors were not. The thoroughness of the search varied, depending on the guards and trusties on duty; and a large amount of the contraband that was later found in the barracks was obtained by prisoners from their visitors.

One man told me that his family always brought a gallon jug of martinis. The guards must have noticed that he always left the visiting area considerably wobblier than when he'd entered it, but he was an old timer with a good record and they let him get by with it.

I was walking on the athletic field near the visiting area that day when Marilyn, Kelly, and Jenny drove up. Marilyn told me later that I must have jumped three feet off the ground when I saw their car. I took off running for the wire fence.

Marilyn was so excited, she had run half way to the visiting area before she realized she still had on the sloppy bedroom slippers she'd used for driving instead of her heels.

The rule was that a prisoner and his visitor could "embrace momentarily" and "kiss briefly" upon meeting in the visiting area. I didn't stretch the rule because other prisoners and their families were staring at us, and I didn't want to make too much of a spectacle.

Other prisoners were not so cautious. Many of the convicts and their wives or girl friends were engaged in lovemaking that would even have been out of place in the darkened balcony of a movie theater. Some of them had the women's dresses up around their waists and their blouses open. Most of the women were sitting on the men's laps, and I believe to this day that two of the couples—with other prisoners, guards, and visiting women and children looking on in the Florida sunshine—consummated the sex act right there in the visiting area.

I know that many prisoners who were ordinarily fairly docile would become extremely agitated in the days after they'd had a female visitor. Two or three prisoners escaped the prison each month I was there, and in the majority of cases, they left within days after they'd had a woman visitor.

The sexual activity that day was extremely embarrassing for me, especially because of Jenny and Kelly. I tried to keep their attention diverted, but it was difficult.

There was no problem about my convict uniform, as it turned out. The children seemed to take it in stride. They even joked about how "cute" I looked in it.

Kelly put me on the spot when she asked rather loudly, during a moment of complete silence: "Daddy, where are all the mean convicts?"

This brought some hard stares and frowns from some of the other prisoners. But the politician in me rose to the occasion as I quickly responded, "Only the good ones get visitors, honey."

That day seemed to pass in approximately the same time it usually takes an hour to go by in prison. We said our moist goodbyes, then I went back to the routine of being prisoner No. 3759.

On February 17, 1970, I went before the parole board. Everything seemed to be in order.

On March 30 I received word that I would be released the following Monday—not quite five months from the time I had entered the Tarrant County Jail in Fort Worth.

I was not allowed to phone my wife, even on this occasion. As soon as I got the word, I sent a quick letter to her—the shortest and happiest I'd ever sent her. I scrawled the words in large capitals on lined notebook paper:

DEAR MARILYN

I MADE IT, MY RELEASE DATE IS APRIL 6—
NEXT MONDAY. OUR PRAYERS WERE AN-
SWERED. I LOVE YOU.

BILL

20

I LEFT EGLIN AFB PRISON April 6, 1970. I had served five months and a week of my year-and-a-day sentence.

As the day of my release approached, I found that my thoughts were not at all what I had imagined they would be. In the early days at Eglin I had often thought ahead to the time when I would be allowed to leave, and in my mind it had always seemed a period of almost delirious anticipation.

But as the actual release date came nearer, a feeling of uneasy dread rooted in me, and nothing I could do—no dreams of freedom that I could conjure up—could dislodge it.

After all those days and weeks, I had become adjusted to prison life. It was regimented, it was dehumanizing, it was nerve-wracking, but in prison at least you were protected, sheltered from the criticisms and expectations of those on the outside.

The prison routine had in a relatively short time done a thorough job of instilling guilt in me. I had been convicted of a crime, and I had been dishonored and punished for it. Now I had to go home, bearing that stigma, and face up to my family, friends, and acquaintances—not to mention my enemies.

It was a frightening prospect. I was uncertain how I would be accepted. And beyond that was the overwhelming task of rebuilding my life again from rock-bottom. I had to re-establish myself as a man—as a family man, and as a man involved in the business and social life of my community.

It scared me to think of it. I had serious doubts about how successful I might be.

As the day of leaving came closer, I began to realize also for the first time just how much compassion I felt for the other men there, all those I'd soon be leaving behind me. True, the majority of them had given me no reason to feel anything toward them other than fear or disgust, but I had developed an understanding of how they got to be the way they were. I had come to realize that with a slightly different background, a less loyal family, a few bad breaks along the way, I could have been in the same situation as any one of them.

Several of the men got out of bed at 4:00 a.m. April 6 to say their goodbyes and wish me luck. I wished them the same.

The prison gave me $25, a suit of clothes, and a bus ticket to Atlanta. I took the $25 and a little more that

Marilyn had sent me and bought a plane ticket. The bus trip would have taken eighteen hours; the plane would get me there in thirty minutes.

A guard took me to the airport and ushered me onto the plane. Everyone waiting to board saw the uniformed guard and stood back from us, letting us on first. On the plane no one would sit within three seats of me. I thought glumly: What a way to start a comeback.

When the plane touched down in Atlanta, Marilyn, Jenny, and Kelly were waiting for me.

I drove the ninety miles from Atlanta to Macon, the first time I'd been behind the wheel of a car in five months. I felt like a kid learning to handle a new bike.

When we reached home, we found the house crowded with neighbors waiting to welcome me back. At the sight of them, of their obvious pleasure in my return, their encouragement, I began to feel a little more up to tackling the tough job ahead of me.

Sitting down to a meal with my family was deep pleasure for me, something I could never describe in words. Several of my friends stayed around through the meal, and what with the laughing, the talking, the crying, and the eating, the dinner went on for several hours.

The next few days were spent clearing up loose ends relating to business and handling details of my parole. I had already sold my pest control and construction businesses; the remaining minor interests I had in the businesses I liquidated.

I had three days in which to report to my parole officer. I would have to report each month to him during the period of my parole which extended through November 11, 1970, the end of the original year-and-a-day sentence.

Two weeks after I arrived home, I began applying for jobs. Because of the nature of my work in prison, I thought I might be able to get a job in the public schools. I went to see Bibb County School Superintendent Julius Gholson. I told him I had a bachelor of science degree in agriculture from the University of Georgia and that I wanted to file an application for a teaching position with the school system if the Board of Education would seriously consider me.

Dr. Gholson was very sympathetic. "I understand your situation," he told me. "What happened to you could have happened to anyone."

He explained the procedure for acquiring a teaching certificate. That same day I drove to Athens to get a copy of my college transcript, then hand-carried it to Atlanta to the Georgia Department of Education, and filed an application for a teacher's certificate.

I was told that I had not had the necessary education courses in college to merit a professional certificate but I would be given a provisional certificate which would allow me to teach, with the understanding that I would take the required courses for a professional certificate as soon as possible.

But then, when I notified the Board of Education that I was ready to teach, things began to slow down fast. Everyone connected with the school system avoided giving me a decision on whether I would be hired. Two local principals specifically asked the school board to hire me to teach in their schools. Still no decision was made.

I learned that several teachers in the Bibb system had been convicted of crimes more serious than mine. Mine had been really, if any crime at all, a crime against myself. Theirs, in some cases, had been crimes of violence, crimes against others.

I learned that certain political figures in town were putting pressure on the board not to hire me. They believed that I'd leave town if I couldn't get work, and that would have suited them just fine.

I felt the fact that the state board had approved me eliminated any problems for the local board. This approval had already established that I was qualified, capable, and acceptable.

As time passed I made job applications with several companies—companies where, it seemed to me, my prison record should make no difference. Always, in the space in the application asking whether I'd ever been convicted, I would answer "yes." I would try to explain my case in the space provided, but there was never enough room.

I never received a response from any of those companies. So in subsequent applications, I left the previous-convictions space blank. When some of these companies did offer me jobs, I would tell them about my criminal record in the interviews. I would explain that I hadn't felt it necessary to mention my conviction unless they were going to seriously consider me for a job. I would add that I believed my character references and the personal interview would tell them all they needed to know about me.

But each time—and there were several of these occasions—when I disclosed my record, the job offer was withdrawn. The interviewers always explained in almost identical words: "We just can't afford to take the chance."

I was angry and frustrated. Here I was with a formal education, trying to get a job—I would have taken any kind of job, I wasn't particular. I'd paid any debt I might have owed to society—paid it in the Tarrant County Jail and in Eglin AFB Prison. Still no luck. I could easily see how other ex-cons with less education might soon give up, turn again to crime, and return again to prison.

Finally, I went back to Superintendent Gholson.

I told him, "I've come to get an answer on the job. You said you personally would favorably consider me. Now I think it's time you gave me an answer. I'm prepared to accept your word on it, either yes or no."

"I'm just the superintendent," he said.

"That's right. But the board will listen to your recommendation."

He was quiet for a few moments, then appeared to make a decision to level with me. "Bill . . . you've been controversial politically. Not only that—some members of the board just don't want an ex-convict in the classroom. You've got two strikes against you, it's as simple as that."

"Dr. Gholson, I've paid my debt," I said. "I've got to start *somewhere*. I filed my application with the board in good faith, and all I ask is to be treated fairly."

"Bill, I tell you what. I'll let you know something definite—one way or the other—next week."

The following week he called and asked me to stop by his office.

"Three or four members of the board are dead-set against hiring you," he told me honestly. "They're afraid of public criticism."

"I understand that," I said. I knew that the board of education had had its share of criticism in the past few years, triggered by such problems as integration and rapidly rising school taxes.

"I don't want to cause any embarrassment to you or the board or anyone else," I told Gholson. "I just want to know where I stand."

"We've worked out a compromise, if you'll accept it," he said, and explained the board's decision. I could work with the school system's vocational education program—but not in the classroom. I would be an assistant counselor and assistant coordinator for the nursing aide program sponsored by the school board at Central State Hospital, the state's largest mental institution. I would have to drive forty miles to the hospital in Milledgeville each day, and forty miles back.

I told Dr. Gholson it sounded as if the board was trying to get me out of Macon, but that I was in no position
to be selective. "I'll take the job," I said.

I had very little choice. I was broke, and I had four
mouths to feed.

Five years earlier, my financial worth was approximately a quarter of a million dollars. But at the time I
took the job with the school system, my family was living
from hand to mouth. Our savings were nil, and we were
still in the same house only because the company that
held a $33,000 judgment lien against the house had not
seen fit to exercise it. This judgment was in addition to
the first mortgage already in effect on our home.

My trial and appeal—lawyers, witnesses' traveling
expenses to Texas and back to Georgia, related expenses—cost approximately $55,000. But that's only a
slight indication of how the case affected me financially.

My case dragged on for five years. For the last four
years of that time, I drew no money whatsoever out of my
business.

At the time the FHA began investigating the Big
Springs project, it not only terminated payments to my
company for that job, but also cut off payments owed me
for other jobs I had in progress for the government in Sa-
vannah, Augusta, and elsewhere. To this day the government has made no allegation that any other work except
that in Big Springs has not been acceptable. In fact, all the
work has been approved. Yet, as of this writing, the FHA
owes me approximately $30,000 on these other jobs. The

Public Housing Administration owes me about $5,000 on a project at Ochlocknee, Georgia. The Department of the Army owes me from $5,000 to $40,000—the amount is in dispute—for the Fort Knox, Kentucky job.

I've turned the matter of collection over to my attorneys, a move that means that even if the government pays me the full amount owed, without litigation, the attorneys will get half of it.

At one stage of our efforts to get paid, my wife called the FHA contracting officer in Washington.

"How can you hold up payment of $20,000 in a case that involves only $3,000?" she asked. The most that could have been involved at Big Springs, if all the allegations were proven true, was $3,000.

"Why, lady, I can do anything I want to," the FHA officer told her. "I once held up $20 million in a case involving $10,000!"

The government is holding all the high cards, of course. The government has the taxpayers' dollars to pay for its investigations, its legal documents, its witnesses, its procedural and technical requirements. Most defendants have no such resources.

The cost of a legal defense soon runs into thousands and thousands of dollars. Any appeal multiplies the cost. Even if the defendant finally wins the case, he may wonder if it was worth it.

There is no doubt in my mind that the government spent close to a million dollars to prosecute me.

A small businessman, however, does not have the

U.S. Treasury to call upon. He cannot afford to retain a battery of attorneys and accountants to advise him on the multitudinous rules and regulations that cover any work done for the federal government today. Even if he can, and if that advice is wrong, he goes to jail; they don't.

While my case was on appeal, I arrived home one night to find our electricity and telephone disconnected due to nonpayment of bills. That was when I decided I would have to sell Town and Country Pest Control.

During this same period I had to call on the Home Indemnity Company, the insurance company that covered performance and payment on all work my company did, to pay some of my bills. This was similar to a loan; the understanding was that I would repay the insurance company when the government paid me. Home Indemnity took out the judgment lein on my house, which meant that they would have been within their rights to move my family out while I was in prison. They could still do it, right now.

All my other debts I have honorably resolved. I owe nothing now other than household bills, although at one point I could have bankrupted my corporation and walked out with in excess of $200,000.

So I took the job with the school system, and was glad to get it.

On Friday the 13th of November, 1970—two days after my period of parole had ended—the Georgia State Pardon and Parole Board granted me a "first offender's pardon." This restored all civil and political rights taken away at the time of my felony conviction—the right to hold office, the right to vote, the right to hold a state real estate or insurance license, and others.

The effect of the pardon was to wipe my record clean. Officially, it was as if nothing had ever happened.

Officially.

The parole board's action had opened an intriguing door. I could get back into politics.

Everyone advised me against it. I hired a professional team to survey Macon voters and they told me I had little chance to get elected. They didn't tell me anything I didn't already know. But the itch was there, and it had to be scratched.

I announced that I would be a candidate for mayor.

In so doing, I lost the job I had had so much difficulty getting. The board of education told me in no uncertain terms that I couldn't run for mayor and work for the school board, too.

The power structure was supporting my opponent in the Democratic primary, F. Emory Greene.

I still loved politics. And I thought that as mayor I could redeem myself in the public's eyes while doing all I could to repay the community that been so good to me in my business and personal life before the trouble in Big Springs.

I lost the Democratic primary election to Greene, 11,000 votes to 7,000. Greene, in turn, would lose to incumbent Republican Mayor Ronnie Thompson.

So I was again without a job, and finding one had

gotten, if anything, harder instead of easier. Again I went through the ritual of applying and the embarrassment of the rejections.

Three months later I was still without a job, and the little monetary reserve I had built up while working with the school system was long gone. Without much enthusiasm I went to talk to Ellis MacDougall, Georgia's new head of the Corrections Department. I had heard that he had a policy of trying to hire ex-convicts who measured up.

As chance had it, the Corrections Department was getting ready to open a pilot work release program for prisoners in Macon. They were looking for someone to head it up. I got the job.

MacDougall also has a policy of requiring all new employees to spend a day or two in jail. He says it helps them appreciate the inmates' situation.

He and I agreed that the requirement could be waived in my case.

Epilogue

I NOW KNOW that if I had it to do over again, I'd never go on trial. I would plead *nolo contendre* (no contest) and throw myself on the mercy of the court.

If I'd gone ahead and started my prison term without a trial or appeal, I'd be a year or two further along the road to recovery by now, and a lot better off financially.

The fact is, a man accused of a criminal act in the United States is thrown into an outmoded, unwieldy, and unfair system of trial and punishment from which he has little chance to escape unscathed, be he innocent or guilty.

I had plenty of time at Eglin AFB prison to think about prison reform, to see the needs from the inside, to talk with men who knew more about the problems than I did. A number of weaknesses in the judicial-correctional system became apparent to me. And more surprisingly, I found that many of them could be corrected with little effort or expense if the correct officials were willing to take the necessary steps and had the guts to do it.

For instance: In all civil cases, the loser has to pay attorney fees and court costs. In criminal cases, the defendant is always saddled with the major costs. The government has almost unlimited financial resources; the defendant does not. Why not have the government pay the attorney fees and court costs in criminal cases where the defendant is successful? An immediate result would be to make the government more responsible in prosecuting cases. And a defendant would be more apt to pursue his case until a final decision was reached, rather than throwing in the towel because of increasing costs.

The presentencing report on each defendant, furnished to the judge by the parole officer, should be made available to the defendant and his attorney so that any inaccuracies or distortions of fact could be pointed out. Mine contained both.

This report reflects the defendant's arrest record, his business and community reputation, credit standing, and any other data that may help the judge in rendering a just sentence. The idea is good; but the information on these reports is confidential, and is seen only by the judge.

Fortunately in my case the judge had strong enough doubts about some of the information to ask me about it during a recess before sentencing me.

For example: The parole officer had reported that Dr. Ed Watson, one of the persons whose names I'd given as a character witness, had said he hardly knew me but that he understood I was the kind of fellow who would "skin a flea for his hide and tallow." In fact, Dr. Watson was the pediatrician for all our children; we had been in business together, we had been on fishing and hunting trips together—in short, we were very close friends. Either the parole officer had talked to the wrong doctor or he had misinterpreted what Dr. Ed Watson had told him. Dr. Watson later wrote a letter to the U.S. Parole Board, contradicting the parole officer's report point by point.

I had given the parole officer two other character references, and to this day he has contacted neither of them.

The parole officer reported to the judge that I had lied when I said I'd finished at the University of Georgia in 1954, because records showed that I had graduated in June of 1955. I explained to the judge that I had taken my last courses in the fall quarter of 1954 but had not been graduated until the following June because no graduation exercises were scheduled until then.

The parole officer reported to the judge that I'd lied when I said I had taken several entomology courses in college. I told the judge I had taken such courses, and I later had Dr. Horace Lund, dean of the School of Entomology, forward to the judge a certificate verifying this through my attorney.

Nevertheless, the allegations did little to help one who was about to be sentenced for not telling the truth.

The parole officer's report contained such hearsay as a statement that a Macon newspaper had quoted a local Democratic spokesman as saying he understood I was telling my close personal friends that I thought Judge Brewster was going to throw my case out of court. It's a little difficult to answer something like that, and it angered me even to have to try.

These are only a sampling of the misstatements in the report. I believe these errors were responsible in large part for the judge sending me to prison rather than putting me on probation.

Sentences should be more uniform, more consistent. It is unfair for a bank president to plead guilty to embezzling $100,000 and get a two-year suspended sentence, while an illiterate from a ghetto pleads guilty to robbing a service station of $15 and gets five years in prison.

When a parole is denied, the parole board ought to be required by law to give the prisoner specific reasons for the denial. One of the most discouraging things in prison is for a man to try his best to be a model prisoner, do everything he can to earn parole, finally go before the parole board, and then, after months of waiting, be handed a little slip of paper stating only that his parole request has been denied.

Some voluntary system should be worked out so that first-offenders could use their talents to render some civic service rather than wasting away in prison. There should be some way such men could be allowed to aid their fellow man or their country—working in a hospital, perhaps, or serving in a foreign military assignment. Keeping men like Lou Wolfson locked up in prison serves no real purpose, but with his knowledge and talent there is no end to the good he could have done if the opportunity had been offered him.

I agree with Wolfson that the states and the federal government should provide tax incentives to encourage business and industry to employ ex-offenders.

It would be beneficial if every judge were required to spend some time on the inside of a prison before he were allowed to send anyone there. The judges should see with their own eyes just how bad it is. A man can't find the words to adequately describe what it's like—and even if he could, such reports by ex-convicts are usually shrugged off as biased or self-serving.

There should be greater flexibility in sentencing; so that when a man reaches the point where he has been rehabilitated as much as he is going to be, he could be released. There is such a point for every man; and after it has passed, imprisonment can have only a negative effect on him. I am not in favor of coddling lawbreakers; I am thinking of what is in the best interests of them and society as well. I refer mainly to first-offenders, white-collar criminals, committers of non-capital offenses—persons who are not likely to become repeaters, unless they are kept in prison too long and therefore become too embittered.

The prisons would be more likely to know when that point of rehabilitation was reached.

The Bureau of Prisons and the Bureau of Paroles should be taken out of the Justice Department and placed under the Department of Health, Education and Welfare. HEW is more qualified to put the proper emphasis on rehabilitation.

Presently the whole array of government forces involved with lawbreakers and their punishment—judges, prosecutors, prison officials, parole officials—are all paid out of the same pot. It is a conspiracy in principle, if not in fact, which works to convict a man, put him in prison, and keep him there.

In prisons right now, even the best of them, the wardens, guards, and other employees couldn't care less about rehabilitation. They let you know right away that you are there for punishment. They drill into you, over and over again, through a thousand subtle and not-so-subtle means, the message that you are a criminal and that you will never change.

HEW, with its army of qualified social workers, educators, and psychologists, would have no link with the prosecuting Justice Department to deter it from trying to do the possible job of rehabilitation.

It is time prison reform got more than lip service. Attica should have showed us that. We should not have needed Attica to show us that.

With the raw fact that 80 percent of the prisoners released return back to the prisons, the majority of us are willing to admit that the prison system in this country is a complete failure. It is like a monster that has been wounded but staggers crazily, never falling dead; we seem unable to stop perpetuating a failing destructive system.

One of the most disheartening aspects of our prison system failure is that the authorities who have been trained in this field and who dictate the size and shape of the prisons, the monies allotted, the people hired to fill positions, etc., are not bringing about the needed and meaningful changes. . . . Unfortunately, it is the inmates, the offenders themselves, as handicapped as they are, who are forcing and bringing about change. As witness Attica. . . . Why must change come from the bottom up . . . from the helpless and hopeless . . . uneducated, mistreated and tortured ones, rather then from the enlightened, educated and monied?

Perhaps the basic failure of the system is the predication of the proposition that stripping a man of his loved ones, his home, his place in the community and his dignity makes him a willing, obedient prisoner who wishes to do well and is repenting of his sins. This concept or premise is doomed to failure, for those who have nothing to lose will gamble anything.

Inside a prison, the prisoner actually runs the joint and only the strong survive, the weak fall to the prey of the prisoner leadership. Can we really expect that the authorities can reduce crime in the streets, when within their own prisons, with everything within reach, in an atmosphere set up and controlled by them . . . indeed ruled by them . . . there is more lawlessness than we find on the worst ghetto street? This is one of the main credibility gaps and the one that makes the man in the street distrust the law.

I managed to survive the crushing steamroller of justice, even though I have lost my business and still owe thousands and lost years from my life. My family paid the real price by being exposed and scarred emotionally by this experience. Why should an innocent family be punished and suffer because of a conviction? In every case more harm is done to the family and they pay the price in so many ways.

Perhaps I was better equipped to face this situation than the average man who is sent to prison and my family was better able to cope too. What happens to the man and family who is less fortunate? Do we really want this price extracted in our behalf? Was your tax dollar well spent when over a million was expended to prosecute me, more thousands were paid to house me in the torture chamber at Tarrant County Jail and finally, at Federal prison in Florida? Could better use have been made of your tax money, than to have it go for the five months and one week that you paid to keep me imprisoned? Or should some intelligent person within the present system, when this whole incredible debacle got started, have put a halt to it and worked out more equitable justice . . . both for the taxpayer, and me, the offender?

Should the judge have borne the responsibility for his decision, the FHA, or the Grand Jury, or do none of these people have to answer for decisions that go wrong and cost the taxpayer millions? Does a man really get justice when he happens to pull a judge with a reputation for toughness, meting out long prison terms for minor offences on secret and false information, while another offender pulls a lenient judge and draws a lesser sentence for a more serious crime? By the time a man is arrested, indicted, convicted and finally sentenced he has paid dearly even before he enters the prison. He has already been punished to a point that he begins to ask himself if he is indeed as bad as the prosecutor says he is in order to gain a conviction. After a while one begins to live up to the image others have set out for him and while in confinement one has to put up a front of meanness to survive. There is a point when a prisoner needs to be released or the hardening process begins to move in on him and this point in time is different for each individual. The hopelessness and loneliness creates such despair that one falls because there is nothing to look forward to.

Some of the specific things that will help bring about prisoner reform are:

1. Uniform sentencing with quick justice so that society can immediately have its pound of flesh and so that the offender serves his sentence while he can still remember what the crime was.

2. A complete reversal of the dehumanizing of inmates; this process unfortunately also dehumanizes the prison authorities. It helps no one and is probably one of the prime factors involved in recidivism.

3. Breaking up a man's family only means more people on welfare, more confused and damaged children who

are unable to escape the cycle, and indeed perpetuates the very thing that prisons are designed to correct. It costs approximately $10,000 per year per inmate to keep him in prison. This is almost $7,000 over the average income in Georgia. To control a man's natural and strongest drives, that deteriorate into homosexual, sadism and beastiality in confinement, a man should maintain a somewhat normal sexual relationship with his wife. The most important link in rehabilitation is the man's family.

4. Men in prison need to think that time can be spent in a useful and meaningful way and that they can go on to something better when they get out. This will help control the inmate much more than punishment.

5. More careful selection of prisoners who serve together should be made at the moment of their initial imprisonment. Young boys who steal money from a candy machine should not be placed with psychotics. We must have prisons with areas devoted to the mentally ill prisoner, the sick prisoner, and the healthy and emotionally healthy prisoner, and the addict who finds it is easier to get dope inside the prison than outside.

6. Outsiders must be pressed into service to visit inside the prisons. Most county prisons would not be chambers of horrors if ministers, priests, rabbis, parishoners, civic clubs and those dedicated to giving aid to the helpless insisted on entrance. They are paying for these prisons after all and they have a right to be admitted for regular visits. Every trial judge should make unannounced visits to the jails in his district to see for himself

what goes on rather than pass the buck to the marshals and sheriffs to verify prisoner complaints. Chief Justice Warren Burger has called on the bar to become involved in prison reform. To date the bar has shown little or no interest in becoming involved. Every prison today is on the verge of blowing up. One can only succumb to agony so long.

7. A prisoner has a basic right to know everything that concerns him; no secret information should be passed on to the trial judge that could be incorrect; no denial of parole for reasons only known to God. How can we expect a man to correct his failures if he is never told what they are?

8. Every law student should be required to intern in a prison just as medical students intern in a hospital. Law students will one day be representing an offender in court, and if he has seen with his own eyes the inside of a prison he will certainly perform the best defense with less consideration for a deal. Most lawyers become judges. They need to know firsthand under what conditions they remand an offender.

9. We know most problems. We have heard many of them and we shrug our shoulders and say, "What can I do about it?" You can do something about it! Begin in your own hometown and start with your city and county prison (jail). Groups have accomplished amazing things in some cities in the United States. Women's groups are investigating the plight of youngsters and women in prisons, supplying them with lawyers, talking to the prison direc-

tor about needed facilities, arranging for counselling and arranging for the care of children. Law students are going into prisons in many cities to handle problems involving the youthful offenders, and in some cases they have successfully gone all the way to the governor to get permission to get into the prisons. This kind of help gets kids out of prisons quickly and avoids overcrowding. Youngsters, arrested, especially if they are out of town, are almost helpless against the morass of legal technicalities.

If you cringe at the thought of entering a prison, well then force your way into the institutions housing youngsters. These are the spawning grounds for our future criminals. Here is where children are mistreated and abused so as to make it impossible for them to adjust satisfactorily to society. Work with the ten year olds if inmates frighten you.

It is impossible to believe that prison reform will come for the "have's." They have the ways and means of bringing about improvement. If they do not, reform will come from the "have-not's" who will be forced to use hostages and violence, and risk being killed shouting . . . "we're human too," in order to bring about change.

ONE FINAL FACT WORTH NOTING:

On Tuesday, February 23, 1971, President Nixon announced that he was suspending the Davis-Bacon Act—the specific law under which I was originally charged and indicted.

W. E. Laite, Jr.